Remembered Gardens

REMEMBERED GARDENS

Illustrated and edited

by

FERRIS COOK

A BULFINCH PRESS BOOK

Little, Brown and Company
Boston • Toronto • London

FIRST EDITION

"The Garden in the Making" from *My Flower Garden* by Herbert Durand. Copyright 1927 by Herbert Durand. Reprinted by permission of Putnam Publishing Group.

"Gardens That Are and Are to Be" from *Truly Rural* by Richardson Wright. Copyright © 1922, 1935 by Richardson Wright. Reprinted by permission of HarperCollins Publishers.

Excerpt from *Forty Years of Gardening* by Anna Gilman Hill. Copyright 1938 by Anna Gilman Hill. Published by HarperCollins Publishers.

"September 24, 1960" from "War in the Borders, Peace in the Shrubbery" from *Onward and Upward in the Garden* by Katharine S. White. Copyright © 1968, 1970, 1979 by E. B. White as Executor of the Estate of Katharine S. White. Reprinted by permission of Farrar, Straus & Giroux, Inc.

"The Second Garden" from *Making Things Grow Outside* by Thalassa Cruso. Copyright © 1971 by Thalassa Cruso. Reprinted by permission of Alfred A. Knopf, Inc.

"Blues" from *Green Thoughts* by Eleanor Perényi. Copyright © 1981 by Eleanor Perényi. Reprinted by permission of Random House, Inc., and Penguin Books Ltd.

LIBRARY OF CONGRESS CATALOGING-IN-PUBLICATION DATA

Remembered gardens / illustrated and edited by Ferris Cook. — 1st ed.
Garden p.   cm.
"A Bulfinch Press book."
ISBN 0-8212-1992-8
1. Gardens.   2. Gardening.   I. Cook, Ferris.
SB455.3.G36   1993
635 — dc20   92-22117

Bulfinch Press is an imprint and trademark of Little, Brown and Company (Inc.)
Published simultaneously in Canada by Little, Brown & Company (Canada) Limited

PRINTED IN HONG KONG

For Ken

Acknowledgments

By inviting me to their homes and sharing
their plants, my friends have unknowingly encouraged me
to put together these essays. There are too many to name,
but I hope they will accept my anonymous thanks.

I owe a special debt of gratitude to others for leading me
to decorative bindings that I hadn't seen before. Judith Ogus, Joyce
Robins, Mary Jenkins, and Catha Grace Rambusch of Wave Hill
have been very generous with their books. Katherine Powis of the
Horticultural Society of New York, Bernadette Callery
of the New York Botanical Garden, and Walter Punch of
the Massachusetts Horticultural Society have graciously
helped me to locate books and information in their
libraries that I was unable to find on my own.

It has been a pleasure to work with the designer,
Jeanne Abboud, and my editor, Brian Hotchkiss. Jeanne
showed great sensitivity to the inspiration of turn-of-
the-century books, and Brian believed that I was
not alone in loving these somewhat antiquated
but not outdated essays and designs. I
am deeply grateful to him for
his encouragement.

CONTENTS

Acknowledgments / *v*

Foreword / *1*

Content in a Garden, by Candace Wheeler / *4*

Setting the Sundial, by Mabel Osgood Wright / *16*

Painting the Landscape, by Mrs. Theodore Thomas / *30*

A Garden of Lilies and Iris, by Helena Rutherfurd Ely / *40*

The Pergola, by Frances Kinsley Hutchinson / *54*

A Little Maryland Garden, by Helen Ashe Hays / *64*

The First Year, by Hanna Rion / *74*

Retrospect and Prospect, by J. Horace McFarland / *80*

Balance in the Flower Garden, by Mrs. Francis King / *86*

My Garden, by Louise Shelton / *94*

Gardens That Are and Are to Be, by Richardson Wright / *98*

The Garden in the Making, by Herbert Durand / *106*

Our First Gardens, by Anna Gilman Hill / *114*

September 24, 1960, by Katharine S. White / *122*

The Second Garden, by Thalassa Cruso / *128*

Blues, by Eleanor Perényi / *138*

Biographies / *146*

A Note on the Illustrations / *150*

FOREWORD

I GARDEN ON LESS THAN AN ACRE of wet clay ninety miles north of New York City. There is an illusion of space because the house is on a corner of the property, near the road. The backyard runs up a hill to woodland, and the woods climb even farther up the hill and then drop down a cliff. Especially in the winter, when the tree trunks are more visible, and the sun is setting, the light penetrates to our yard, beckoning us to stroll to the last light. Kind neighbors allow us to trespass up the narrow deer trails to a moss-covered stone perch where we have a view of the Catskills.

My husband, my son, and I came to Ulster County quite unexpectedly. We had seen a house for sale in Connecticut, which started us wondering. Although it was beside a polluted river, it was a charming summer cottage with an extensive rock garden. And it was springtime. By autumn we knew of two other houses for sale. In early October we went apple picking in the Hudson Valley and saw them both. The first house was too big, but the second was just right. It was a late-nineteenth-century farmhouse with a nice front porch. There was a barn full of old stuff, an outhouse and sheds, and barbed wire crisscrossing the back field, where horses had been kept. We drove home in silence and made a bid on the house the next evening.

When the previous owner handed over the keys on a gray leap year's day and we went to our new house, we lay down in the snow and looked up. In the first pictures, taken that day, we are motionless angels in the snow.

Little did I know that within a month I would do my first work in the garden. I made a path, and it went straight up to the sky.

Climbing the big pine tree next to the house, I broke off all the dead branches on our living jungle gym. The garden began with such clearing: old fencing and barbed wire were removed so that the field could be mowed. There were lilacs, peonies, and roses entangled with honeysuckle. I planted a few things, but I didn't plan since it was all new: the house, the yard, the trees and flowers. As I identified new plants, they seemed worth planting. So a meandering border with stray flowers, tropical and wayside, became my garden.

✺

When I think back, I remember that by looking for a house, we were looking for more space than the city offered. I, in particular, was looking for a room of my own. But the house was small, especially since it was divided into two apartments. So, for privacy and solitude, I turned to those outdoor "rooms" that garden writers describe. The different places are barely distinguishable from a baseball field, because they run together, but I have given these areas names for easy reference in my notebook: the fern garden, the bench garden, the slope garden, the blue spruce garden, and so forth. As in the house, the contents of the rooms are apt to be moved. But the places where we sit and enjoy the gardens will not change.

In the photo album, the pictures of the garden are side by side with pictures of friends and family. Some loved ones are dead, and some friendships have faded, but I see the growth and maturing of familiar faces as well. In the garden, some of the first shrubs I planted, a buddleia and broom, have already died because I didn't provide enough drainage. The pine trees and spruces planted by a previous owner look small in pictures from the first year we owned the house. And I remember how huge the vegetable garden was the second year. Every year I widen all the flower beds, but the pine branches grow faster than the garden expansion. Soon my "pine tree garden" will be moved as the tree conceals the garden beneath.

Each garden's history is unique. One of my friends lives where there was once a summer camp. The feeling of a camp lives on, as she and her family occupy five cabins, in one way or another, and her garden surrounds the original stream-fed, rock-lined swimming pool. Lining the stream are masses of woodland and bog plants that lead into terraces of flowers around the pool. Another friend lives in an old train station and gardens on the narrow strip of land where the train tracks plowed through the woods. Columbines of every size and color obliterate the rectilinear shape of the clearing. Still another friend gardens in the center of town, on a shady fifteen-by-twenty-foot backyard, while another lives in an eyebrow colonial house at the top of a hill. In all directions are sweeping vistas of the Shawangunk and Catskill mountains. Her huge delphiniums and rhubarb are intermingled with hundreds of poppies in the biggest flower bed. Such diversity within a ten-mile radius encourages many visits and plant exchanges. Despite our sharing of seeds and the entwining of all our gardens with poppies, our gardens bear little resemblance to each other.

Through all of this, and through getting to know fellow gardeners, I have discovered that to invite someone to reminisce about his or her garden is to encourage odd details: unknown plants, unmet friends, and tales of former structures and rebuilt homes. The interest is not always the floor plan or the landscaper's map, but the sequence of planting and building and the telling of the story. The conglomeration of details out of which the current garden grew is a collection of memories. And gardening is about remembering what has been done, what needs doing, what things look like, and when flowers bloom. While every year I forget to send birthday cards, I can remember to divide the meadow rue and the painted ferns. My own garden memories are part of a tradition, and the essays in this volume are the stories of small adventures and great beginnings.

Ferris Cook
High Falls, New York
December 1992

CONTENT
IN A
GARDEN

by
Candace Wheeler

1901

MY GARDEN OF CONTENT lies high on Onteora Mountain. It is a half-round space of rough red soil, sloping to the east, and inclining upward and inclosing the log studio.

When I began to dig and plant, I little knew the joy which would grow out of the soil, and descend from the skies, and gather from far-off places and times to gladden my soul; but to-day, as I walk therein, or sit in the spicy shadow of its pair of fir trees, and think what it has done for me, I feel that untroubled happiness begins and ends within it; that it is truly the Land of Content.

It was just a rocky patch of pasture land lying between us and the woods, when it came into my mind to plant it as a garden, and how could I guess that the ground of it had been longing to blossom? But when I saw how it received and fostered and urged into growth the things I planted, I understood that the earth mother had coveted the power of making herself beautiful.

Before the garden was made, there were two young balsam-fir trees growing almost under the house eaves, — young things pulled from the roadside in one of our drives. It was easy to see that they approved of the garden, for summer by summer they threw up yard-long blue-green spires, until now, as I stand on the upper piazza, I can hold a cup and gather their drops of balsam.

How fine they are! Just at the college-graduate age, and full to overflow of the joy of living.

There is something in a balsam-fir which seems to gather to itself almost more than its arborescent share of human interest. The young trees are delightful babies; one can hardly walk away and leave them alone. Just as innocent and enticing as a human baby, and appealing to sense as well as sentiment, for they exhale the sweetness of a freshly-bathed one-year-old.

Their behavior is ideal! Would that human childhood might stay in its own place, and do so exactly what one could wish, as do the young balsams! Their youth and middle age are almost equally satisfactory, but when they come to *old* age, sorrow for the first time enters their lives, and strikes them with a too early decrepitude. Indeed, the age of a fir tree is wholly wanting in the royal beauty and dignity of an aged oak, or even a venerable beech tree. The blood of youth sinks away into the soil, the sinews dry into powder, and leave the brittle limbs no strength to battle with the storms. But I refuse to look forward to old age for my two lusty fir trees, — now at least

> *"God's in His heaven:*
> *All's right with the world."*

Two other live species my garden contained at the very outset: an apple tree, and varied clumps of the wild pink mountain azalea. Now, in late May and early June, when the garden is in fullest flower, this dear apple tree, just grown to full maturity, stands at the garden edge and showers shell-like leaves over it all, and the pink azaleas, from their places here and there among the purple iris, lift each a glowing torch of color to the spring.

There is hardly in the world a tint exactly like that of the wild pink azalea. It is not made of a mixture, as are other pink flowers, where you can trace vermilion and crimson and scarlet pulsing through the grains and veins of white. It is all pink, deepening into crimson in the curving stamens, contrasting perfectly with the young green of its folded leaves, and smelling of the very essence of spring, of roots and mosses and wintergreen and partridge berry, and all that makes spring intoxicating to sense and spirit.

When I began to plant, I found I must build some kind of discouraging barrier between my precious half acre and grazing horses and straying dogs. Not a fence; for a fence would be incongruous in the face of the near woods and far mountains and the heavenly slope which begins at the garden, and, flowing off for fenceless miles, at last reaches the Kaaterskill Clove, and is lapped into the blue distance of the Hudson Valley. So it happens that because we do not mean to cut ourselves off from careless nature by careful civilization, the garden ground is rimmed with a lengthened stone-heap which does not separate it too positively from the rocky slope of which it was originally a part. In truth, it is not a wall, but a rolling up and circling around of boulders left in the track of a former glacier.

When one looks at the landscape, it is not hard to imagine a great ice sea streaming through the deep mountain hollows, and creeping, creeping, creeping over the slopes toward its final dissolution, grinding all the rocks into fragments of broken uniformity! After the glacier came the forests of beautiful evergreen giants, but that race also has followed the glaciers into eternal vacancy. Standing among my flowers, the aeons of time are all within the compass of a thought. Glacial days, when the world was shaped with an ice axe; forest days, which sheltered unimaginable prehistoric beasts; later days of primitive man; and after them all the days of to-day, when my garden smiles and smells. My own little day, so full of love and joy and sorrow and contentment!

When I inclosed my garden, I meant that the wall should be broad enough to grow weeds and grasses and blossoming stone-crop on its top, for nothing has ever seemed to me more beautiful than the springing of grasses and flowering weeds on gray stone walls. Any one who has seen wild oats poising their wave-green heads against the blue of an English sky, growing between buttercups and crimson sorrel along the sills of high-up empty windows of English cathedrals, or has watched the transparent glaze of scarlet poppies trembling along the brink of Roman ruins, must long to see again the grace and beauty of green growths on old gray stone.

It is an effect we do not often get in our dear new country, where the very stones — except when one finds them in deep old forests — seem absolutely new; as if they were created yesterday. And yet they are old, as old as the world; it is only we and our work that are new. Yet I did not see why, by a judicious filling in of chinks and hollows with turf, I might not patch the new effort upon the old, old stone, and so compass my heart's desire of a growing wall.

It does grow, in a measure. Not quite as I willed it; but whoever has not learned to let Nature have her way is not fit for a gardener, or, for that matter, for a contented soul. So the stones of my wall are not entirely covered, although outside it grows the wild white clematis, and inside, the sweet striped-honeysuckle. Twice in the summer it is an irregular mound of blossom and sweetness.

I have so planted my garden that the flowers come in procession, each month or period with its own special glory. To make this summer procession a perfect one, I have taken care that while one kind of flower is passing, it shall occupy all the garden with an unbroken sheet of bloom. Thousands of flowers of one variety, lifting their faces to the sun in the morning or standing on dress parade through the afternoon, make an impression upon the eye and the imagination which is impossible to mixed masses, however beautiful their separate parts.

In a large and new garden it is not quite a simple matter to secure this breadth of effect, but with time and care and parsimonious hoarding of every wandering rootlet, it is easily possible. When I acquire a new variety by purchase or gift, and there is not enough to plant broadcast, I put it in the nursery. This is an indiscriminate flower bed absolutely sacred to my own care, where I plant parted roots and seeds and cuttings of anything of which I am avaricious; and having planted, encourage them with kindness and tendance, until each has made a family after its kind. When any one variety has multiplied largely, I consider its color and time of flower, and decide what it will harmonize with or what it shall follow; and so, upon a settled plan of flower decoration, I plant it everywhere.

If, on the other hand, one must buy flowers for planting, — which to a real gardener seems an unnatural proceeding, and to one of long experience an unnecessary one, — it is as easy to buy by the thousand as by the dozen, and a certain sentiment will attach itself to a thousand tulip bulbs, which you know were grown on the mud flats of Holland, tended by slow and heavy men in blue blouses; and after they were grown and harvested, ferried along low-lying canals to some sea city, there to be gathered into innumerable thousands and shipped to America. As you scatter the thousands over your garden ground, each into its own little pit in its own little place, you can see in your mind the flattened fields of their nativity, covered with millions of blossoming tulips, and the grass-edged canals along which slow boats are creeping, and here and there a group of red-tiled roofs, pointed and ruffled, and accented with small dormers. All this you see because you bought your tulip bulbs by the thousand instead of the dozen; and yet you will not love them as you would inevitably do if you, your very self, were responsible for their growth and increase.

But there are flowering things in the garden, even before the early-rising bulbs. One or two wild things lead the rest. Before even the daffodil has made ready to blow its golden trumpet, all along the borders the bloodroot is spreading its transcendent silver stars, and the green-striped sheaths of the star-of-Bethlehem are opening.

These came from the pasture corners and open woods of Long Island, where they have attended strictly to the business of their own maintenance, and gone on growing in spite of the change in proprietorship of the land from copper-colored nomads to Dutch burghers, and after them by process of evolution to the Long Island farmer with his thorough methods of cultivation; yet even he fails to eradicate the tubers of the bloodroot, or the closely bound clumps of tiny bulbs which flower out into the star-of-Bethlehem.

And after them come the larger bulbs. First of all the daffodil, coming up before the frost cracks have melted together in the ground; sending up their crowded spikes with a wonderful concentration of purpose, — and almost while you watch them, one of the seeming leafy blades will swell into a bud and urge itself on, up and above the others, until it stands confessed a daffodil bud all yellowed in the sun, and ready to open its flower in the night, when no one can see the mystery of its birth.

I find myself especially interested in bulbs. The small, compact round which I hold in my hand in the spring includes such a variety of possibilities! If it has been turned up in the border by the spadingfork, it may be an ascension lily, or a Canadian lily, or a scarlet wood lily; and the little bulb knows where it belongs, though I do not. I cannot tell what sort of blossom it carries folded within its layers, and what it will become when its growth impulse is awakened. If I put it back into the ground, I may be blindly planting it out of accord with its surroundings; for at this stage of its being it looks a bulb and nothing more. I do not know its nature by its shape or size or color; it keeps its individuality for summer days.

And there is the same difficulty with the lesser bulbs. Tulip and daffodil and narcissus are twin sisters or triplets, and one of them astray may be anybody's child; therefore it often happens that where I look for narcissus blooms I find daffodil, and where I expect a cluster of daffodil spears a single broad tulip leaf will appear, guarding a central bud.

One of the wood walks of our Long Island homestead borders a long swale of black mucky ground which, in the days before the Brooklyn waterworks were, was a sluggish brook and a ferny swamp. It came to me to utilize this place by transplanting into it the army of poet's narcissus which regularly every spring budded on the lawn in millions, and later shriveled in millions, if the spring rains were not copious enough to satisfy their thirsty souls. And this plan answered beautifully. The narcissus sent up its spears of buds dutifully, and when they came to the bursting point, the swampy ground was, and is, every recurring spring, covered with a blanket of creamy white blossoms. But something else has happened. The first spring after they were planted, and buds began to show like sharp green bayonets along the rows, here and there I found a plant with longer leaves and fatter buds. Presently these outstripped the others, and opened into double daffodils; and spring after spring they have increased, making clusters of themselves in the rows, until now we go down to pick daffodils early in May, and narcissus some two weeks later, from mixed masses of yellow and white blossoms. It seems, then, that when bulbs are in question we sometimes reap where we have not sown.

It is a pity that daffodils ever took it into their heads to grow double. Some one of them at some time in flower history must have had a double tulip for neighbor, and seeing it turn out its bunch of magnificence to the sun, said in its heart, "I can do that," and straightway began in a hurry to grow inner leaves, and has continued to do this until the golden trumpet is crowded out of existence. They are not perfect leaves, by any means; half of them are stained with the green of the calyx, and half are of an intense yellow which is almost orange, not at all the true daffodil color. I miss and regret the beautiful ruffled-edged trumpet; but taken as it is, the double daffodil represents as perfect a determination to grow and *be* as I find in any flower save the orange day lily.

The single daffodil is not so persistent as the double, and, in fact, I am tempted to believe that it is naturally an ambitious flower, and changes its style from pure determination to do all it can in the way of what one of my farmer friends calls *blowth*. If it could know, down in the depths of its single heart, how fascinating its trumpeted flower can be, it would surely keep itself single. The very poise of the flower-head is the perfection of grace, and to watch an early cluster stand swaying upon their individual stems is to fancy they are like a group of nymphs, each one more graceful than the others.

The daffodil and narcissus, which are really blood relations, are the most prolific of flowers. If I plant a single bulb, it will not be long in gathering a family, and in the course of two or three years the spot in which it grows will have become as populous as the tents of the patriarchs. Its clustering habit makes it a convenient bulb for transplantation. I need never search for separate ones in the flower beds. When I come upon them, there are hundreds packed so closely together that I peel them off like the scales of a pine cone; and each separate one I plant will make itself into another clump if I give it time. It is not so with tulips; their little rootlets run off and start a bulb at a greater distance.

In the fall or spring I fill my marigold and nasturtium beds with tulip bulbs, which, being early risers by nature, get up and blossom in the spring days in great beauty, while the dormant speck of life in the marigold and nasturtium seed is just beginning to be conscious of an awakening thrill. I can fancy that through July and August and September days, when the summer flowers are rioting above them, the buried bulbs are quite as contentedly busy underground, living a hidden domestic life and adding children to themselves by dozens. Perhaps, — who knows? — they feel a sort of placid burgher contempt for the untimely activity of the seed plants that adds a stronger flavor of contentment to their own quiet days.

When I see them in May preparing for this peaceful underlife, I feel like blessing them with Herrick's song "To the Daffodil," and saying to them after him: —

> "Stay, stay,
> Until the hastening day has run
> But to the even-song,
> And having prayed together, we
> Will go with you along."

I am quite sure that the apartment-house fashion I have adopted of planting bulbs and seeds in layers is agreeable to both; since they make no sign of disapproval, but go on, each doing its best in its own flower season to cover the ground with blossoms. It is a convenient fashion for the gardener, since spaces bare of either foliage or bloom suggest insufficient love or inefficient labor, and either of these would be out of harmony with the cheerful power and grateful joy which reign in every well-kept garden.

After the daffodil comes the poet's narcissus; and after this, suddenly the garden is a garden of tulips; and by that time June has arrived, and it is the time of the iris; its variations of purple and lavender, and the bluish pinks and pinkish blues which tend toward those colors, are mingled in a crowd of stately blossoms which stream in radiating rows to the garden's outermost verge. Then a border of golden lilies encircles them, and outside of these a mound of scented honeysuckle hides for the time its purple-lined leaves under trumpeted flowers, and the growing sprays go wavering up in air in search of invisible fibre by which to climb. At this time I am apt to think that the very limit of garden beauty has been reached; that in the summer procession I have planned, nothing can be so beautiful; and yet, all the while a detachment is on its way with its own special glories of color and costume. The tightly packed apple-shaped buds of pink peonies are beginning to show streaks of color, and when the latest of the fleur-de-lis has blossomed, and the purple banners which it had flaunted are dried and shriveled in the sun, the spaces between the radiating rows are filled with the deeply lobed leaves of peony, and the globes of buds are opening into scented flowers, each one like a separate bouquet too heavy for its stem. The great pink globes roll from side to side like heavy-headed babies, and the garden becomes a mass of rose color set in green. I have planted meadow-rue between the clumps of pink peony; and their long stalks, bearing foam-white flowers, push themselves among the great pink blossoms as if they were intent upon furnishing the proper creamy setting for this mass of bloom. This deliberate juxtaposition on my part is the result of a happy accident of combination. Some one coming in with a handful of meadow-rue gathered along the roadside, thrust it into a piazza-jar filled with pink peonies, and the effect of the two dear opposites of beauty, the softening of the one and intensifying of the other, gave me the happy thought of planting them next each other. Although of such different natures they grow happily together, the bud-stalk of the rue threading a path to the light between the heavy green of peony leaves with judicious dexterity, and the roots love the soft garden mould, and seem to revel in unaccustomed ease of growth. They send up new leaves until late November, making inviting little cushions of columbine-shaped green, when nearly every other growth has succumbed to frost.

These two make a long step in the flower procession; they usher in white lilies, and the summer pinks which are ready for their places. How, I wonder, does each flower of each species know its time so inevitably! Nothing can hasten, and nothing retard it; no seduction of summer-like spring days can bring it forward, or blustering of fall-like summer days delay it. When the time set for flowering by the far-off forbears of its race has come, it flowers. Surely such steadfastness and persistence, if given to man, would carry poor wavering humanity far on its way to accomplishment!

SETTING THE SUNDIAL

by
Mabel Osgood Wright

1901

NOVEMBER 1. Last night I told Evan my plan of turning the old strawberry bed into a bit of formal garden, and he agreed that it would be a natural resting place for the eye in its journey from the seat under the apple tree down the walk and across the fields.

He emended the somewhat crooked design that I had traced on a slate found in the attic desk, and made me a fascinating water-colour sketch in which the strawberry bed appeared as a small level lawn in the centre of which stood the sundial acting as the hub to a large, wheel-shaped flower bed, or rather, group of beds, as the wide spokes, each of a different but harmonizing colour, were separated by narrow grass walks. A similar walk circled the spokes and was bounded in turn by a circular bed that might be called the tire of the wheel, and divided the grass walk into four in order that one might get to the centre without walking through the outer bed. Four graceful wing-shaped beds filled the corners of the grass plot, which by actual measurement proved to be forty feet square. This plateau was on three sides enough higher than the surrounding ground to allow an arbitrary grass slope of two feet, with a couple of steps where the long walk joined it.

Without suggesting what plants should be used, — that is to be settled on some dreary day in midwinter when the first seed catalogue appears, bringing its tantalizing mirage of possibilities, — Evan washed in a colour scheme that he knew would satisfy my rather savage taste, and make this formal bit a blaze of light without the aid of a single "foliage plant." For it is really astonishing how few colours are inharmonious when they are profusely massed and have green for a background.

One thing we decided about my Garden of the Sun, as Evan calls this formal bit, because it stands out in the open entirely without shelter. It is to contain only the perishable summer flowers, really flowers of the sun, and fit companions of the sundial. Gorgeous blossoms that come into being in June after the hardy roses have vanished, and glow and blaze until they fairly bloom themselves to death, before the frost touches them.

Of these flowers some are annuals, and others tender perennials or so-called florists' flowers that it is always a mistake to mix with bulbs or hardy perennials, for in the early season they are overpowered, and in their turn choke the hardier plants, exhausting the goodness from the soil by their rank growth.

As for the spring bulbs, I do not like them in set beds, each of a kind, and arranged in stripes or figures, any more than I do the formal beds of foliage plants. Grown in this way, as soon as the bulbs are out of bloom they must be replaced, or the space will look ragged and unsightly. This does away with the natural seasons of the garden. I think that one of the greatest charms of nature to women is that she is, like ourselves, a creature of moods, phases, seasons, and not always equally radiant.

Her wild garden has its spring, summer, autumn, and winter seasons, one waxing as another wanes. I think the cultivated garden should follow the wild plan, and while it must yield flowers in some part during the whole growing season, it ought not to be coerced and stuffed like pâté geese and every bed expected to be in full bloom at all times.

Besides, this constant pulling up and replanting entails labour not within the power of the commuter's wife, who, if she is wise, plans as far as possible for the permanent, so if she is obliged to neglect her flowers for a time, garden baldness will not result.

Evan says that if gardening is to be my relaxation and a pleasure, I must pursue *it*, but be very careful that it does not get the upper hand and pursue me, for he has seen this turning of tables not only cause the downfall of many gardens, but of country homes as well.

✤

If, a few days ago, Cris had put the sand where he was directed, I should have planted my bulbs in the wrong place. During the delay Evan discovered that the grassy stretch outside the study and windows of our den, where Father tramps to and fro and smokes when he is thinking, looked bare, and something was needed to shield the foundation of the house.

This is a dry and sheltered nook, and an ideal location for bulbs, if they are planted well forward of the path and drip-line of the eaves. Evan has marked out two curving beds that follow the line of the path that goes to the rear door, and I am massing all my bulbs in them, — daffodils, narcissus, hyacinths, tall late tulips, the golden banded auratum, pure white madonna (*candidum*), and pink and crimson spotted Japan lilies. I shall plant them in groups, not rows, according to height rather than colour, so that by scattering some portulacca seed in June, the ground will be covered beneath the tall stalks of the later flowers, and we shall have colour under the windows from April until October. There are no plants more healthy, sturdily brilliant in bloom, and unlikely to disappoint than the bulb tribe.

These are the only two flower beds to be allowed out of strict garden limits, as we have decided that all the other decorations grouped about the house must be tufts of eulalia, various shrubs, and groups of scillas, daffodils, peonies, and iris set in the grass. The older shrubs we have in plenty, great masses of lilacs, syringas, and snowballs filling every corner and overarching the walk.

Our ancestors were aided by their usual common sense regarding economy of labour, when they gathered their little home gardens in a corner, often fencing them in from the rest of the land. Here the flowers could be considered as a whole, be loved, tended, watered, and protected from insect enemies without waste of energy.

Upon this same principle I must collect my flower family under one roof, so to speak, keeping them in such order that I may not only enjoy them freely, but minister easily to their needs quite out of the range of highway criticism. Not that I object to being seen weeding, watering, tying, and insectiding in a perspiring and collar-less condition, but I do not wish to be pounced upon by every patient that calls and be expected to take them into my sanctuary, there to prowl and despoil me of garden privacy or flowers after the custom of the idly curious. It is something of a responsibility of course to be one's own gardener, but an infinite satisfaction withal to feel that the making and even the marring is within one's own grasp. That is, as far as things agricultural are ever within the power of a mere human. For as a humbling and God-fearing occupation, none can exceed the gardener's. Mother Earth has ways of trying and proving the temper or lack of it that cannot be surpassed for variety.

As I look back over the years that I have watched garden processes, and sown and gathered my little crop of flowers, it seems that I should now know enough to keep clear of cultural sins both of omission and commission. Yet when I realize all the things that are uncontrollable, I turn pagan and am inclined to make a series of shrubby grottos to harbour the deities of Sun, Rain, and Seasonable Weather, so that I may secretly propitiate them with offerings. It was a woman gardener who said feelingly, "Paul may plant, but if Apollos declines to water, what can one do about it?"

In these days, however, all well-conducted dwellers in the country have artesian wells and windmills, and are thereby able, up to a certain point, by means of a diamond spray sprinkler, to sneeze in the face of so important a person as even Apollos himself.

Of course we have one of these wells, both for outdoor convenience and because Father has been trying for many years to convince the community that neighbourliness does not require them to drink each other's drainage. This they do inevitably on the village and river side of the hills, where wells and cesspools alternate with great regularity. Surely the country life is the healthiest in the world, otherwise the rank and file of people who live it would never survive the liberties they take with themselves!

※

This morning when Father, Evan, and I, followed by Tim and Bertle, arrived at the garden a further surprise was ambushed behind the rose arbour, in the shape of two men from the florist over in town of whom Father had bought my birthday flowers.

"You see, Barbara," said Evan, shaking hands with himself behind his back, a manner he has of expressing satisfaction, "people

always call in extra help at a 'house-raisin',' so I thought that I would do the same at this 'garden digging'; for if your beds are shaped now, you can in your mind's eye plant and replant, until when spring comes everything will be decided to your satisfaction."

I laughed aloud and clapped my hands at this new outbreak of one of Evan's strong traits; for the dear fellow had only a few moments before warned me that I could expect to do very little until spring, at the very time that he was providing men with stakes, measures, and lines to lay out the garden without delay.

Making a noise when I am pleased is another of my savage traits. Animals do it; the dogs bay with pleasure when invited for an unexpected walk. When good luck came to Toomai of the Elephants, he sat out in the night and thumped a tom-tom in pure joy. Civilization is mostly silent in happiness, feeling doubtless that at least feigned indifference is expected of it. I often wonder whether we gain or lose by being civilized. It is so much less complicated to be a savage.

❦

The next consideration was the location of the sundial, for a hole must be dug and a rough foundation of stones, rubble, and cement laid before it could be set.

Fortunately the strawberry bed had been carefully levelled in its youth; the ashes used as a top dressing, drawing white clover to fill the place of the departed berries, promised very respectable turf, that by a careful weeding out in spring and raking in of fresh seed would serve quite well. After Evan had driven the central stake Bertle set to work with his shovel, advised and admonished by Tim, whose dialect Scotch must have seemed a weird language to his Danish ears.

Meanwhile Evan and I strolled up and down the long walk rather perplexed how to proceed, while Father surrounded by dogs watched us from his seat under the tree, and the two extras stood at "rest arms."

The borders, about six feet in width, were a hopeless jungle of hardy plants interspersed at intervals with shrubs and tall bushes of the older roses such as Magna Charta and Jacqueminot. Some of these met over the path and partly barred the way. At this season of course the hardy plants could be distinguished only by their leaves, and being herbaceous, any night a hard frost might destroy even this clue.

There was a broad band of hollyhocks too well placed against the honeysuckle bank to be disturbed, straggling helter-skelter were foxgloves, Canterbury bells, larkspurs, phloxes, sweet William, columbines, white anemone Japonica still in bloom in company with monkshood, hardy coreopsis, evening primroses, honesty, and sunflowers, while the autumnal growth of white, yellow, and red day and tiger lilies and scarlet oriental poppies was distinguishable.

After several turns up and down in a brown study, Evan threw back his head and cried: "I have it! I will have the men grub up all these plants with the exception of the roses and shrubs and put them on the walk, work over the beds thoroughly, and

dig in good old manure from that heap in the field. Then the plants can be reset neither in a jungle nor in stiff lines, but in groups of a kind between the shrubs, which really, when properly trimmed, will make a series of alcoves to break the awkwardness of straight lines. Some shrubs are too old and must come out or be replaced, and others, like the great syringas, lilacs, and snowballs, can be allowed to meet over the walk and may be cut out to form natural arches. This I will manage myself. What do you think of my scheme, Madam Commuter? Doesn't it keep the old and yet put it in a tangible, workable shape without breaking any of the canons and laws of my craft?"

I said that it was charming and suited me exactly, but did not add that it was precisely what I myself had planned yesterday in the attic and sketched on the reverse side of the old slate. It is a great mistake to collapse the lovable little self-conceits of men, for they are of a wholly different quality from egotism. Besides, to have told Evan that his plan was "piper's news" or that "great minds think alike" would have deprived him of the pleasure of pleasing me. Poor Aunt Lot had this fatal quality of forestalling surprises and caused me to lock up the characteristic for future avoidance in my brain cabinet.

Then Evan called the men, and the digging and sorting began. It will take them at least a whole week to restore these hardy beds to order, but luckily the "extras" are a birthday gift and do not have to be recorded and extracted, or I should say subtracted, from godmother's fifty pounds. Though really I suppose I should credit the garden account with them, all the same, if we are to keep track of what it costs. But why keep a garden account and reckon the cost of pure joy? Is it not cheap at any price?

But, on the other hand, if I do not keep the realizing sense of cost before me, I may be tempted some day to write a delusive book upon how to run a country home, horse and cow inclusive, on ten dollars a week, supply a family of ten with vegetables grown in a city plot, or give minute instructions as to the way a cripple may support himself by raising roses for market from cuttings obtained from withered bouquets, in a greenhouse glazed with castaway photograph plates and heated by a kerosene lamp!

I may not be wholly sane in my regard for money. In childhood a dollar did not mean a hundred cents, but twenty packets of flower-seeds; ten cents, a clump of pansies, a verbena, or a small geranium; while twenty-five cents stood for a heliotrope, a Fuchsia, or a tea-rose in forced and consequently hectic bloom. Even now money never seems an actuality unless reckoned by its products, merely being according to its volume, — so much food, so many plants, dogs, books, or a coveted bit of land or a horse, consequently a commodity not to be hoarded but to be immediately sent out to fulfil its destiny. For as long as you keep money it yields nothing but worry, the current rate of interest being simply beneath contempt. On the other hand, you buy dogs and you buy food; one eats the other, there is no waste, while satisfaction and good company is the result. Also you buy seeds and manure; the seeds eat the manure, and flowers are the results. Is not this true economy?

Evan shakes his head at my theories, and yet when I corner him, he confesses that he has somewhat the same feeling and that the ideal condition to him would be to work for pure love of it, never thinking of money, but simply by putting the hand in the pocket always finding the sum necessary to pay for the article purchased.

❊

This morning as we walked to and fro, hatless and absorbing the wonderfully balmy air that Father said was a reprieve granted to autumn by summer in honour of my birthday, we crossed the open square and followed the line of the cart track down the field among the trees, until it wound in and out like a cowpath.

"We might," I suggested, "use this cart track as a walk through this short stretch of smooth ground and end it where the bushes and trees begin, continuing the beds of hardy flowers beside it. Some

day perhaps we will have this old wood lot ploughed up and cultivated.

"Cultivated? No," said Evan, as if an inspiration had seized him,
pointing over the half-dozen acres where the children of the ancient
wood in the shape of second growth hemlock, maples, a few beeches
and red oaks mingled with dogwood, cornel, bayberry, sweet fern,
and hazel bushes, and the dry yellow fronds of the cinnamon and
bleached hay-scented ferns grew amid a maze of seeded asters and
goldenrods that still showed here and there a fresh spray of yellow.
"No, this shall be your wild garden. A strip of a made path here
until it curves under those hemlocks, then merely a grass trail of a
lawn mower's width running where you will, and to be varied
according to mood, until it reaches the bars where we will have a
bench and stile. Ferns there are already in plenty, and we can bring
fresh roots home from every back-country trip we take. The wild
things will never mope and starve in these surroundings; so we need
not cultivate, but merely adjust ourselves to the land."

"Yes, and the spring hole with the mossy cask around it, where
the cows used to drink down by the bars, we might use for a lily
pool and have Japan iris and native water plants in the surrounding
muddy ground. Oh, Evan, you angel, for a long time I've suspected
you of having nice, strong, practical, magic wings folded away under
your coat. This thought opens possibilities not even shadowed in
my Garden of Dreams."

"It is for this and the wherewithal to make your dreams come
true that I am here instead of in that older garden overseas. No,
don't look distressed, sweetheart; for after all, a man's wife is his
home and kindred."

Then Father came up, wondering what we were discovering either
in each other or in what, to unilluminated eyes, seemed only a
ragged wood lot, brown with November's smoke tints.

When we had explained that the Garden of Dreams was to begin
at the "Mother Tree" and end quite out of sight in a maze of
wilderness, his face was strangely lighted, and putting an arm

around my waist and Evan's shoulder, he drew us together, saying, "Children, your lives, I believe, will be a long walk through the garden of your affections, and your old father thanks God that he is allowed to walk even a small part of it with you."

☙

The hardy roses and shrubs that Evan had bought also as a birthday gift to supplement those we already had, have been banked up in the vegetable garden until the borders are rearranged. Of course we take a risk in planting things so late. October is a better time; but if we have a close snowy winter, there is little danger, and we shall put straw jackets on the roses until they are established. On the other hand, if one waits to plant hardy things until spring, the ground may be late in thawing, and a whole season's bloom lost.

How delightfully the damp earth around the plant roots smelled when Evan unpacked them this morning. I think I must have a tinge of poor Peter Schmidt's love of the soil, irrespective of what it produces, in my nature, for the various earth odours all have a separate tale to tell, and the leaf mould of the woods bears a wholly different fragrance from that of the soil under pasture turf, or the breath that the garden gives off in great sighs of relief when it is relaxed and refreshed by a summer shower.

This happy birthday has held two sensations not in the planning and planting scheme. When we were sorting the bulbs, the hounds carried off the bag of snowdrops, and after worrying it, ate a portion of its contents. Without looking in either Dodoens's or Gerarde's "Herbal" for the medicinal properties of snowdrops, I now know that they give puppies severe colic. Fortunately Bugle and Tally-ho did not eat many, and Evan secured the rest and has bedded them in a spot unknown to me, so that some early spring day I may go out and be surprised by finding them.

I also have planted a surprise for Evan in the grass bank at the foot of the honeysuckle tangle, a spot where the sun lies warmest in March, — half a dozen tufts of yellow primroses and cowslips taken from the Somerset garden and smuggled home in a box of moss deep in a trunk cover. If they thrive, he shall have a bank of them in time, for I saved plenty of seed.

The second happening was more serious. The sundial was to be placed early in the afternoon with some little bits of sentiment, by way of dedication. The foundation was completed, and the shaft, a simple, rather graceful vase-shaped column, set in position. Martha came out, and looked solemnly on at a respectful distance, taking no notice of the somewhat crookedly admiring glances of Tim; for Martha is not unattractive, having good hair and a portly freshness not seen among our farming women of fifty or thereabouts.

Father and Evan were busy with compass and level; but though the sun shone brightly, the shadow cast by the quaintly wrought brass finger would not fall in the right place. Alack! the difficulty could not be adjusted; for owing to differences in latitude, an English-born sundial cannot tell New England time.

Father laughed mischievously as he rallied Evan upon the inadaptability of the race to which he was the exception that merely went to prove the rule. Evan did not laugh, but as he glanced at me, we mutually recognized each other's right of birth, and the dial will stand as a safeguard to remind us to respect each other's patriotism.

Meanwhile, Martha Corkle gave a suspicious sniff, and remarked,

"Crossin' seas don't change the 'eart," while Tim forgot himself and indiscreetly clapped her on the back, saying apologetically, "Who'd ken the puir dumb stane 'ud be sa obstinate?" a proceeding she resented by stalking into the house.

However, the dial is set, and will add a meaning to the garden of the sun that shall surround it. Mother, who went away in the long ago, I'm so happy to-night, that I am sure you are very near. I seem to feel your arms, and I know that you also understand.

PAINTING
THE
LANDSCAPE

by

Mrs. Theodore Thomas

1 9 0 4

ELSENGARTEN, AS I HAVE SAID, is situated halfway up the slope of a mountain. The cottage stands on a broad terrace in a large clearing which we purposely keep free of trees in order to command the full sweep of the superb mountain view to which I alluded in a former chapter. The Wise Ones tell us that the view would look better, the mountains higher, and their colouring brighter, if we would interrupt the horizon here and there with a splendid tree. But to me its greatest charm is that I can see the whole stretch of eastern sky clear and free, without having to crane around big tree trunks, or peer through branches for both ends of the rainbow, when there is one.

Ah, those rainbows, how glorious they are! Nothing in the way of scenery could be more enchanting than one of those great gleaming, double, and sometimes triple, arches of coloured light, resting on billows of verdant tree-tops, overshadowed by threatening thunder-clouds, and framing within their shining arcs the rock-crowned peak of Lafayette — now a transparent purple wraith, the mere spirit of a mountain, glowing softly through a veil of mist! True emblems of hope and promise, the blacker the tempest lowers above them the brighter smiles their steadfast gleam. I should be sorry indeed to have that sight broken in twain by even the best of trees.

Hence, our clearing is kept free of trees on that side of the house. But, although trees are banished there, nature is allowed a free hand with other growths, and lavishly has she taken advantage thereof, and filled it with grasses and ferns, goldenrod, hardhack, asters, fireweed, everlasting, yarrow, and I know not how many other wild and luxuriant flowering plants. This ever blooming wilderness is, however, not brilliant, but, on the contrary, its tones are low and rich. Its greens are olive, its yellows tinged with brown, its reds incline to purple, and its whites to gray. On the upper edge of this wild open space is the little plateau where stands the cottage, and here we have allowed ourselves the luxury of a well-kept lawn, and the pure, fresh green of this, contrasting with the turkish-rug effect of the wild part, is very cool and pleasant to the eye. Above this, again, is the stone wall, with its brilliant mass of cultivated flowers, set like a jewel amidst the encircling green, and still farther above is the sombre line of the forest rising tier above tier as far as the eye can reach. . . .

The masses of bright colour placed here, with the granite of wall or ledge jutting through, is very effective, and harmonizes with the wilderness around as the oasis harmonizes with the desert. Little by little I added other beds, large or small, to the vicinity of the cottage, until I decided that I had reached the right proportion of colour, and that more flowers here would detract from instead of adding to the beauty of the picture.

It is always a temptation, when seeds sprout, and runners put forth from precious shrubs, to save the healthy little treasures by enlarging old beds, or adding new ones to the garden space. This is all right where one has a real garden, but, in the sort of garden I am telling about, it is very easy to ruin one's effects instead of heightening them by too much decoration. It is like fussy trimming on a dress, and, if one has nobody to give the little plants to, then one must ruthlessly dig them up and throw them away, and sternly resist the temptation to enlarge the floral masses beyond the limits of artistic proportion.

The dominating idea in the cultivation of Felsengarten has been to keep it as nearly as possible as nature made it. In planning its walks, its little pond, its grottos and rustic benches, and in the treatment of rocks, woods, springs, and other natural features, it was our endeavour to produce nothing which was not already there, but to enhance, as far as our taste and judgment allowed, the natural features of the location.

Thus the Meister, in planning his avenues, followed the natural indications of the land. The woods were cleared of unsightly rubbish, and trees pruned, or cut out only where they crowded each other unduly. Otherwise they were left wild. The weeds and overgrowth on ledges and boulders were cleared away, and an occasional touch of rugged stone exposed, and — highest triumph of all — the rank, ugly swamp was metamorphosed into a charming pond, with brook and waterfall.

This last was no small achievement for one unused to engineering problems, for the little hollow where he wanted that pond to stay was by no means at the bottom of the mountain, but only at the bottom of our part of it, — a very different thing, — and the water had no intention of standing still in our pond when it was only halfway downhill! But the Meister is gifted with the grace of continuance, and when the water leaked out of his pond overnight, after his cohorts had been working for weeks to dam it in, he patiently recalled them for a fresh start, and had the dam built all over again. Three times the brook was diverted from its course, the pond dug deeper, and the heavy masonry of the dam strengthened, and then at last the water gave up the struggle and yielded itself an unwilling prisoner; and that which had been the most hopelessly ugly part of the place was transformed into its very prettiest spot. It was suggested to the Meister that he could stock his pond with trout, and add the much-needed variety of an occasional dish of them to our somewhat monotonous mountain fare. But he would have none of this. "What!" said he, "first feed a creature, and then eat it? — I do not like that idea. I wish one could get on without this everlasting killing and eating of meat, but, since that is not practicable, let us at least not devour our friends!" So the pond still remains untenanted by fish, but other kinds of live things seem to have taken up their residence in it, with the result that we often see little poachers in fur or feathers untroubled by any such scruples of conscience embellishing *their* dinners at its margin!

With the exception of the pond, and some of the very heavy chopping and clearing, the work of improvement on our place has been done by the Meister's own hands, with rarely any other assistance than that of the "Handy Lad," so often mentioned in these pages (who, by the way, has grown up into a clever young man since he first appeared in them). And, with no other teacher than nature and experiment, the secrets of forestry and landscape architecture gradually revealed themselves to him, as those of planting and growing came to me, and after a while he evolved a very simple and practical method of planning and carrying out his improvements.

Before leaving Felsengarten in the fall, he would select the locality he meant to improve the following summer, and wander over every inch of it until he was familiar with all its features; and its trees and boulders, humps and hollows, and general topography were "photographically lined on the tablet of his mind." During the winter he would plan his improvements, and the following spring he was ready to put them into execution. First he would clear the section of rubbish, ragged growths, inferior trees, dead branches, and other unsightly objects. Then he would stake out the path or avenue to be constructed, and, beginning at one end, he and his young assistant would work at it quietly, day by day, and as the work progressed the embellishment of the adjacent land naturally suggested itself.

When all was completed to his satisfaction he would call me, and, indicating with an expressive sweep of the arm some shady nook or sunny clearing, would remark, with a confidence in my powers which fired ambition, "Put red colour there" or, "No red here, but dark blue and gold." And then I would take up the work in my turn, and try to paint in the desired colour with flowers. It was not always easy to put "red colour," nor yet "dark blue and gold," in the places indicated, for they were often spots where none of the reds, blues, or yellows of my acquaintance would consent to blossom. But there was nevertheless a certain excitement about experimenting, and much instruction evolved from each effort. It was as if Dame Nature had said, "I dare you to put it there." And, whenever I got the better of her and succeeded, it was a victory indeed, besides introducing me to new flowers, or teaching me about hitherto unknown traits in the old ones.

In all my plantings, however, the dominating idea was to make the flowers look as if they had grown there of themselves, and as I thought nature might have placed them had she been inclined. In the large beds of cultivated flowers near the house, this, of course, was impossible, for nature never decorates in quite that way. Therefore I was careful to set these beds in an environment of lawn, — which is also an artificial, and not a natural growth, — and the combination of colours in these flower masses presently came to be very carefully considered in the endeavour to produce a well-balanced and perfectly harmonious series of colour schemes from spring till fall, so arranged that as fast as one set of flowers faded another would blossom in its place.

Many a struggle has this idea of colour combination cost me. I had no thought of it at first, and planted recklessly everything I could lay my hands on, anywhere a patch of unoccupied ground offered it a resting-place, quite regardless of what the ultimate size, shape, or colour would be. And it was not till they were full grown and began to blossom that I discovered pink phloxes and orange tiger lilies engaged in hand-to-hand combats of outraged colour, and other equally trying combinations. And by that time many of the shrubs were too old for transplanting, and I had to pull them out and throw them away. One year a hydrangea and a hardy larkspur, by some hocus-pocus of nature, blossomed in each other's embrace, making such a charming confusion of mingled blue and

white that I longed to duplicate the effect. But, although I planted a dozen larkspurs beside as many hydrangeas, the two never blossomed simultaneously again, but did so seriously incommode each other, and get into each other's sunshine, that I was soon obliged to move them into another location. Indeed, the blossoming season differs so much in different years with us, that it is necessary to leave a wide margin in calculating for colour combinations. And I even question if it would be possible anywhere to count upon the blossoming season of hardy plants definitely enough to plant artistically till one had practically tested the locality, and planted and replanted until the grouping was determined by actual experiment. Soil, moisture, altitude, climate, and even the variations of different seasons, all affect the blossoming time of shrubs and plants. It would, therefore, not be of much help to those living in other localities for me to name the plants grouped together in my beds, because these same plants might elsewhere blossom at different times. For the same reason I have found it advisable, in buying plants from a florist, to buy from one whose nursery is either near by, or, at least, located where the conditions are similar as to climate. For they are more likely to fulfil the promises of the catalogue if they are raised in the same kind of a climate as the one in which they will be expected to grow.

If, however, I cannot suggest the special groups which blossom simultaneously in my garden, I can say in a general way, that in a cultivated border the same laws of form and colour can be applied as a basis of arrangement that are used in any form of decorative art. The most satisfactory results in colour are those in which the proportion is approximately one of yellow, to two of red and five of blue. Or, one of white and three of pink, to five of light blue. In either case the primary colours should be blended together by many times their combined quantity of tertiary colours — green, gray, etc. The secondary colours, such as purple, orange, magenta, lilac, etc., can be classed as modified primaries. But it must be remembered that the relative brightness of these colours is not the same as that of the primaries, and due allowance must be made in proportioning them. Orange, for instance, is more vivid in the border than pure yellow; but magenta does not compare in brightness to scarlet, nor lilac to blue. These two colours, magenta and lilac, are best planted in rich masses, combined with a great deal of white. I have no combination more beautiful than that of hydrangeas flowering side by side with the pale little lilac wild asters of our northern fields. This little aster, by the way, which is charming even under the most adverse conditions, is luxuriant in a cultivated border. Each plant sends up a dozen or more stalks three feet high, which are covered with such a riotous mass of fairy flowers that they look as if enveloped in a cloud of lavender foam. A group of these plants blooming beside a gray boulder with a snowy mass of hydrangea overhead is a garden picture worth having.

In the repetition of groups, again, as in the proportion of colour, it is safe to apply the rules of decorative art, for one must have balance and proportion in form, as well as in colour, to make the picture harmonious. At the same time care must be exercised in the repetition of the groups to avoid making the border into a mere stiff piece of "carpet gardening," as it is called.

These are the problems that every garden-maker has to work over and solve for herself, nor, I fancy, will she ever find herself so wise, or her garden so perfect, that each successive fall and spring will not find her moving something somewhere, and experimenting with a new something in its place!

It takes many a failure before one discovers the road to success, but it is sure to be found in the end. And what a proud moment it is when the owner of some famous garden — one of the truly "wise" — casts an approving eye over one's simple efforts, and exclaims, "How beautiful your flowers are!" and perhaps asks for a root of this or that plant! I do not know anything which instils into one's inner consciousness a more serene sense of contentment than this subtle form of flattery! But in gardening, as in all other pursuits, it is always the connoisseur who sees the good points most quickly and touches most lightly on the shortcomings, and nothing is pleasanter than to wander about the garden with such an one. Not only is he appreciative of what has been done already, but, as he walks and talks, he gives forth many helpful suggestions for future touches here and there, or imparts little practical secrets concerning easy ways of achieving results for which we have vainly laboured.

Equally pleasant is it to make a return visit and see with him his splendid domain, for nothing of all its beauty escapes the eye trained by a little experience, and one enjoys and learns at every step. How jealously one looks at his specimens of the plants that are in one's own garden, to see if they are better grown and bear larger flowers than those at home! And with what immense satisfaction does one spy out those which are not so good. Alas, poor human nature! Must the green-eyed monster invade even the sacred precincts of our very gardens? I fear it is even so, and confess that the very first thing I did on reading of a garden where the blossoms on the phloxes measured more than a silver dollar, was to get a silver dollar and measure one of mine, and it cannot be denied that the result produced much cheerfulness of heart.

The exchange of seeds and plants which always attends such garden visits is one of the pleasant incidents connected with them. My garden is a veritable album, and as I wander over our place I find many a dear friend or happy hour commemorated in it. This little clump of oxalis, naturalized so prettily in the woods, was gathered one lovely day when a merry party joined us in an expedition to the Profile Notch. That group of lady's-slippers came from the woods of a dear friend in Vermont. Here are moss roses from a magnificent rose garden in Massachusetts, and there are seedlings from the home of Longfellow, or willows rooted from cuttings brought from the South by Frederick Law Olmsted. Hardly a flower-loving friend have I who has not left an autograph in plant, or shrub, or tree in my garden, and in like manner many a thrifty plant has left my borders for those of distant friends.

A
GARDEN
OF
LILIES
AND IRIS

---

by
Helena Rutherfurd Ely

1 9 0 5

SOME YEARS AGO I heard of "A Garden of Lilies," a garden where nothing else was grown. The phrase and the description of this garden remained in my mind and the desire to have one where Lilies particularly should be grown took great hold of me. In my imagination I saw the tall, graceful stalks crowned with their beautiful flowers, cut the lovely things and breathed their delicious perfume. After reading all that I could find upon the cultivation of Lilies, and studying the catalogues, I finally made a beginning.

The place where I planned to have this garden had been for years a garden where small vegetables had been raised. The ground sloped slightly towards the southeast, enough to continually wash the top soil to the foot of the slope, which was partly corrected by terracing; the soil was hard and clayey and had never made a very successful vegetable garden. The first thing was to plan the best arrangement of the space.

Some time before, a friend had given me a plan of her garden, which was old when the Revolutionary war was ended. Washington and his officers had walked there, and for the hundred and thirty years that had passed since those days the place with its beautiful garden had remained in the same family, loved and cared for in every generation.

This old garden has the formal-shaped, Box-edged beds seen in all Colonial gardens. The Box, tall and thick, entirely fills the beds in some places, and the bushes of old-fashioned Roses, Paeonies, Madonna Lilies, and many of the other old-time flowers have grown on, increasing in size and beauty, while generations who have tended them have followed each other to their last long sleep.

The straight Box-edged paths, and the formally shaped beds surrounded with Box, are found in all of the early gardens, the idea having been brought over from the old country by the colonists who planned their new gardens here, after the manner of those they had known and loved at home, and grew wherever possible the flowers they had tended across the sea.

The English and early American formal gardens were a modification and simplification of the elaborate Italian gardens, where architectural structures, tall cypress trees and ilex and myrtle hedges were the principal elements.

To many persons who have never been gardeners themselves, or studied the pleasing art, all formal gardens are Italian gardens, and since making this new one I have spent much time in explaining, that it is not an Italian garden but a Colonial one, designed from a garden made in America about 1760.

Having longed for the sound of falling water among the flowers, it seemed that now was my opportunity; so a pool, round, twelve feet in diameter and three feet deep, was planned for the center of the garden. First the place was excavated and the water pipe and connections with shut-off valve and back drainage put in place; then a wall of stone about eighteen inches thick was laid up in cement, the bottom concreted and the overflow pipe laid to a loosely stoned-up blind cistern made below the level of the bottom; this also served to drain out the pool in winter, the water soaking away through the loose stones into the earth.

The pool finished, the surface of the entire garden was covered with a thick layer of manure, on which was spread about three inches of muck taken from the bottom of a pond that was scraped for the purpose. Lime also and sand were added to mellow the stiff soil. The ground was then thoroughly ploughed, harrowed several times, spaded and carefully raked. Then with stakes and garden cord the beds were marked out, and again spaded and thoroughly prepared, the whole garden again raked, and the place was at last ready for planting. The pool was begun in early April, but various delays made it the end of May before the garden was finally laid out. The beds were surrounded with Box-edging and many pyramidal evergreens planted.

On June the fifth, the space between the beds was sown with grass seed, an unheard-of date, and as it was too late to think of Lilies for that year, the beds were sown the following day with Asters.

For seven weeks there had been no rain, and, worse still, no wind, and the wind-mill did not pump and the great reservoir supplying the gardens became dangerously low. Early in June I sailed away for Europe in a sad state of mind, begging the men to cart the water if necessary to keep the Box and evergreens alive.

Scarcely did I dare all Summer to think of this garden, and no mention of it was made in any letters received, so that upon our return the middle of September I went to look at it, expecting to see a bare expanse broken by dead evergreens and brown Box-edging; but the rains had begun the very day we sailed, and the Summer had been cool with frequent rains.

It was just sunset when we reached home that September day, and as I stood on the marble steps, looking down upon what my imagination had portrayed as a dead garden, it seemed as if a miracle had been wrought. The evergreens were green and flourishing, the Box-edging was covered with tender shoots of new growth, the grass of the paths was thick and free from weeds and the beds were filled with blooming Asters, of which there were certainly hundreds in each bed, and although three colors had been used, white, palest pink, and faint blue, each bed contained but one variety. In the pool the *Nelumbium speciosum* spread its great blue-green leaves and two of its pink lilies with golden hearts rose on tall stems above the water. The pale colors with the fresh green setting seemed in the soft sunset-light almost unreal after the sad expectation that had so long filled my mind. Any garden lover will sympathize and understand my great delight.

In October, when frost had killed the Asters, the beds were finally prepared for the Lilies and Iris which they were then to receive. Over each bed was spread a layer each, of old manure, leaf-mould, bone meal, wood ashes, phosphate, and a sprinkling of air-slaked lime, the beds were then spaded and re-spaded so as to mix the new constituents thoroughly with the soil already there, and then came planting time.

But for a moment let me digress and again say a word upon the preparation of the soil, for in this lies the great secret of success in gardening. Make it deep and rich and light, giving to the plants the food they require, and, with weekly cultivation and an occasional soaking to the roots if the weather be dry, you cannot fail to have a successful garden.

People continually ask me, "What is the use of making the beds so deep?" and "Why not put the enrichment on the top of the ground?" If you make a garden with beds but a foot in depth, the plants may struggle along for a year, but look at them the second year and see their stunted condition and poor bloom, and in comparing such a garden with one properly made, the answer is found. If there is a foot of good rich soil *below* the roots of the plants and all the rest of the earth is equally good, the plants are enabled to resist a drought that would otherwise cause them to cease blossoming, and in ordinary weather to reward the gardener with a wealth of bloom. Good garden soil, with some sand to lighten it if too heavy, and plenty of old stable manure are all that need be used for the garden. But for a small garden a bag each of bone meal and phosphate, with some wood ashes occasionally used sparingly, will help the plants along surprisingly. Anyone can make leaf-mould, which is a valuable addition, by saving the rakings of the Autumn leaves and turning them occasionally until the following Autumn, when they may be dug into the beds. I do not intend to touch the soil of my Lily and Iris garden for at least four, and possibly five, years, beyond giving it every year a mulch of fine manure or leaf-mould when the plants are well up in the Spring.

All Lilies will flourish in rich loam to which a good proportion of sand has been supplied, and once planted, they should not be removed as long as they are doing well.

But if the leaves fall from the stalks and the bulb seems unhealthy, it should be carefully dug up, any part of the bulb found in a bad condition removed, the bulb dried with a soft cloth and shaken in a paper bag containing powdered sulphur, and replanted immediately. Miss Jekyll recommends this use of sulphur and I have tried it with good results.

It is always a problem how to arrange a garden so that it may be flowering from May until frost, and here were seven large beds to be filled with Lilies and Iris only, and yet kept blooming throughout the season. Of *Iris Germanica* there were pure white, pale yellow with violet markings, yellow and brown, and various shades of purple and blue; the lovely "Madam Cherau," white with a frilled edge of light blue; many varieties of Japanese Iris, white ones predominating, however; Florentine Iris and the English variety Mont Blanc, both of these also white; Siberian Iris, white veined with yellow, and also violet ones; Spanish Iris, growing tall and stately and bearing flowers of wonderful coloring. The foliage of the Spanish Iris is so like the wild onion that I was filled with alarm when I saw the beds in the following April and immediately dug up a bulb to satisfy myself that a crop of onions had not appeared by magic; and, last of all, Chinese Iris, but this did not bloom, although flourishing and green, with foliage quite similar to the Germanica.

The different varieties were laid out on the floor of the tool room, divided into seven parts, and then planted in the seven beds, some of which were larger than others.

Of Lilies there were *Auratum, Speciosum Album* and *Speciosum Rubrum, Longiflorum, Brownii, Batemanni, Krameri, Leichlinii, Rubellum, Chalcedonicum, Excelsum, Superbum, Wallacei, Canadense,* and *Hemerocallis,* the yellow Day Lily, in all eight hundred Lilies and five hundred Iris.

The Lilies were divided into seven parts like the Iris, and each bulb was set in sand, a foot in depth, and the small varieties from four to six inches deep. Some were planted in clumps of one or two dozen of a kind, but the rarer and more expensive varieties had only from four to six in a group.

The names of the Lilies somewhat phased the men. I asked one the name of the bulbs on a large package he had just laid down. After a moment's study, he replied, "Oh, they're the Long-i-fellows."

The last of November the beds had a heavy cover of coarse manure. I was afraid of stable litter or leaves, for fear that field mice might burrow in and eat the bulbs. Then came the terrible winter with a degree of cold which that wise person "the oldest inhabitant" described as unknown in his lifetime, and with it the fears that little in the new garden would survive. But the kindly snow spread over all a warm white blanket, which remained from December until March. The garden was uncovered the last of March and by mid-April the beds were green with the shoots of Iris and the bronze-green of the stout Auratum Lilies, and every sunny day new plants appeared to see what the world was like.

A lady sent me some bulbs which she called "Brazilian Lilies." These bulbs were planted the end of April among the other Lilies. They came up shortly and grew rapidly, beginning to bloom about the end of May and continuing for three weeks. The flowers are quite different from any I have ever seen, the heart of the Lily being pale green shading to yellow, with yellow anthers, and each blossom has five outside petals with fringed edges. The bulb also is unlike other bulbs, being of a consistency between a Bermuda onion and a beet. They are tender, requiring to be stored like Gladioli during the Winter. After blossoming, the plant makes a beautiful foliage that in itself is most ornamental. I wish I knew where these bulbs might be procured, as they are the greatest addition to the Lily garden.

Tiger Lilies are not grown in this garden, but flourish and increase on the edges of shrubberies and along a stone wall, which latter place seems to be their natural habitat.

The lovely Candidum, too, has no place in this garden. It does not like our soil or my treatment, and after buying hundreds with scant success I have abandoned their culture.

The German Iris began to bloom on May 20th and continued for three weeks. The Florentine and Siberian Iris both began to blossom on May 25th and shortly after these came the English Mont Blanc. By June 10th the Spanish Iris unfolded its first blossom, dark brown with a tinge of purple and a dull gold heart, and one day the third week in June the first Japanese Iris, white with a golden ray through the center, appeared to bid me good morning as I walked through the garden; I cut the last of these Japanese Iris the 3rd of August.

The fragrant yellow Day Lily, *Hemerocallis florham,* was the first Lily to open its petals in the new garden, about the 25th of May, and bloomed freely for about two weeks. Next to begin blooming after the stranger from Brazil were the lilies Krameri and Rubellum, which appeared about June 15th. They are quite alike in form, foliage and color; the latter a soft pink, like the lining of the conch shells we have seen on mantels in farm houses, treasured reminders of the distant sea. Next came the Auratums, on July 4th, surprisingly early, for elsewhere on the place they did not appear before July 20th. This, however, gave us the Auratums for nearly two months, as the last one was cut about September 1st.

At the same time Canadense, a native Lily, began to flower and was disappointing, as it bore less freely than those growing wild in the meadows of the farm. The wild ones, however, grew on ground that could more strictly be called wet rather than damp. The Canadense has two varieties, flavum yellow and rubrum red. Each bulb bore from three to five lilies.

While the Auratums in the lily garden were in their prime, the Longiflorums unfolded their white trumpets and were beautiful for three weeks, and before these passed away the Lily Brownii appeared, growing on stems about three feet in height, with one or two trumpet-shaped flowers, in form like the Longiflorum. These lilies are white on the inside, the outside shaded with brown and purple.

They were followed the third week in July by the Chalcedonicum (the scarlet Turk's Cap), a lily of the Martagon type. These lilies grow in a small cluster at the top of stems about four feet high.

They are not large, only three inches across. At the same time the Japanese Lily, Wallacei, began to flower. It is apricot in color, spotted with brown and very large, and has generally but two lilies on a stalk; the stalks are not over three feet in height.

The Lily Batemanni bloomed first on July 25th; it has flowers of a warm shade of apricot without spots, growing generally in groups of three blossoms, on stems about four feet tall.

Lilium Leichtlinii, a Japanese Lily, also bloomed during the first ten days of August. I found it very beautiful and delicate, of a pale yellow color, with purple markings on the inside. The stems seemed frail, and although one or two bore two lilies, there was generally but one on a stalk, and I fear that this Lily will not bear another year.

Superbums bloomed all through August, and the petals of the last one fell the very end of September. The stalks are about five feet in height and each stalk bears certainly twenty lilies. I am told that this variety, when well established, increases in quantity of bloom until there are often thirty flowers and the stalks eight feet high. The flowers are crimson-orange and remind one of the Tiger Lily.

The middle of August, while the stately Auratums still lingered in the Lily garden, the lilies Rubrum, and Melpomene which is quite like Rubrum but more brilliant in color, and the beautiful wax-like *Lilium album* appeared; and, of these, the ones protected from the frost did not cease blooming until the second week in October.

One other Lily, Gigantium, said to grow six feet high, was planted, but not in the garden. It required "a cool woodland," according to Miss Jekyll, so a corner was found under tall trees where Rhododendrons formed a background; a large place was dug out and filled with specially prepared soil, and, with a petition to the goddess Flora, the bulb was carefully planted, only one, because they are expensive — three dollars apiece — and this was an experiment. Three weeks, a month, five weeks, went by and no sign from the bulb. Impatience could no longer be restrained, and with care it was dug up. Alas! the bulb was nearly gone. The soil or climate or something was unpropitious, and thus I was unable to have the handsomest of all the lilies.

By the first of June every inch of space in the beds was filled with Asters, Gladioli or tuberous-rooted Begonias. Each bed had one of these varieties of flowers.

These Begonias, which are a most beautiful flower of waxy texture, quite four inches across, were started in hot-beds the first of March, began to blossom in early July and continued until killed by hard frost. The bulbs may also be planted in the open ground in May as soon as danger from frost is over. Plant with the hollow end of the bulb up, and cover with two inches of earth; they will begin to blossom early in August. Both the foliage and the flowers are beautiful, and they are so easy of cultivation, that no one will regret having them. They prefer a partial shade, but when given a mulch they do perfectly in full sun. The white are the handsomest; afterwards the pink and scarlet.

In the Autumn the bulbs should be taken up, after the foliage has been destroyed by the frost, carefully dried and stored through the Winter. It is a frequent practice to pack the bulbs in boxes of dry sand, the bulbs not touching each other, and then to store the boxes in some suitable place, but for the last two Winters I have kept them in baskets in an ordinary cellar, side by side with similar baskets of Gladioli, Dahlias, and Cannas, and they have been in perfect condition in the Spring.

The Begonias began to flower early in July, the Asters and Gladioli the middle of August, and all continued to bloom until the frost came.

Other than Lilies and Iris, this one annual and the two summer-flowering bulbs were all that were admitted to this garden. To observe the Iris and Lilies as they came into bloom was most interesting, but of the many varieties of Lilies there are, after all, but few that are entirely satisfactory, and fewer still that can be counted on to increase. Of the latter there are the *Speciosum album* and Rubrum, which last thrives best in a partially shaded location, or if given a heavy mulch can be grown in the sun; Canadense, Superbum, the Tigers, Krameri, Rubellum, and the yellow Day Lily. Beautiful ones which we cannot do without and yet which disappear after more or less time, are the Auratums, Longiflorums, and *Brownii.*

The old-fashioned Funckias, called "Day Lilies" by our grand-mothers, require too much space to be admitted to the Lily garden, but are grown in masses elsewhere, and I often wonder whether the clusters of slender white trumpets or the great yellow-green leaves are most beautiful. Funckias, like the Paeonies, should be undisturbed, and for the first two or three years not much should be expected of them; afterwards the number of blossoms will increase every year.

In the pool there were *Nelumbium speciosum*, the pink Egyptian Lotus, a tender Water Lily. If the season is early they can be planted about May 15th. Fill a flower tub or butter tub, which must first be made perfectly tight, with equal parts of cow manure and garden loam which have been carefully mixed. Contrary to common opinion, it is the soil that nourishes aquatics, not water. Plant the Lily roots nearly at the top of the tub, covering only with about two inches of soil well pressed down. If a bulb or shoot has formed, be careful to allow it to project above the soil. Finally cover the earth with about two inches of sand, which prevents the soil in the tub from discoloring the water. If you have no pool or pond, the Nelumbium or the English Nymphaes or our native Pond Lilies can readily be grown in a kerosene barrel sawed in half and sunk in the ground to the rim, in some effective place where it will have full sun, generally in front of a shrubbery or with a background of low evergreens. Half fill this with soil, plant the Lily, not forgetting the sand, fill up with water and from time to time replenish the water to replace that which has evaporated.

Water Lilies are beautiful alike in flower and leaf. The delicate petals of the pink Nelumbium with its great golden calyx, the flower when extended being quite twelve inches across, and the velvety leaves often measuring twenty-two inches across, the first to appear resting on the water and later ones rising on straight stems two feet or more above it, make this plant an object of unusual beauty. Nothing can be more interesting than to watch its daily growth.

Every few feet around the pool, just back of the wall, English Ivy is planted, which as it grows is fastened down with hairpins, those most valuable implements of femininity, and will, it is hoped, in time surround the edge of the pool so that the water will be framed in green. The ivy can be protected in Winter by a covering of leaves and some evergreen branches. In the pool are several varieties of fish, among them goldfish, which not only add to its beauty, but devour the larvae of the mosquitoes which otherwise might breed in the fresh water.

Many birds nest in the gardens: blackbirds, robins, gray wrens, the faithful phoebe birds, who return year after year to the same nesting place, and raise two families every season; orioles, whose nests hang from the branches of the tallest trees; yellow birds; meadow larks; humming-birds innumerable, darting from flower to flower with lightning-like rapidity; black and white woodpeckers with scarlet heads, which live in the tall old locusts and share these trees with the blue-jays, which are always at enmity with the robins and also fight the red squirrels to preserve nests and babies. Last year a pair of quail nested among a mass of Phlox, and later went away to the upland fields with eight plump, well-grown little ones.

These birds have appropriated the pool as their favorite bathing place; alighting daintily upon a great leaf of Nelumbium, the crystal water in its hollow forms their bath, and from a little distance you may see them dip and splash and then alight upon a nearby branch, or upon the tall stalk of a Lily, and preen and dry their plumage before flying away into the blue.

Americans with houses in the country are learning to live more and more out of doors; to take book or sewing or writing to some quiet, retired spot in the garden under a shady tree or arbor; to see their friends among the trees and flowers, and there have afternoon tea or take an evening meal *al fresco*.

In our garden a bench near the pool is a favorite resting place with all. There is a dreamy fascination in listening to the splashing water, whose liquid tones lend an accompaniment to the thoughts that flit through the mind even as the shadows flit across the hills, or the changing clouds are reflected in the water. At night when the tall white Lilies gleam through the darkness and the air is heavy with their perfume, and moon and stars are mirrored in the clear pool, it is the time and the place for "touches of sweet harmony," and when a pure voice is heard singing "and the night for love was given, Dearest, come to me," from Schubert's serenade, a final enchantment descends upon the spot.

When staying at Oxford and wandering through those grand old gardens it has been easy to understand how their calm beauty and charm have inspired the thoughts of the men who have produced so much that is best in English literature and poetry. The shaded alley by the Cherwell, the great purple beeches, the shadows fleeting across the grass, the antiquity of the place and all that the great university has stood for in its centuries of existence, these surroundings and the life in the gardens must, if there is any poetry or spirit of imagination in him, stimulate the Oxford man to valuable literary work.

THE
PERGOLA

by
Frances Kinsley Hutchinson

1907

ROM THE OUT-OF-DOOR DINING-ROOM, following the outline of the house, extending along the west side of the lawn, runs the rustic pergola. Built from the trees which we had been obliged to cut, their bark left on, the larger ones for the posts sunk four feet in the ground and placed ten feet apart, the smaller ones for the roof projecting three feet on either side, it did look at first quite bare and hopeless. As a neighboring farmer put it: "A nice lot of wood you have there, but I shouldn't say it was piled real economical."

This arbor, two hundred and fifty feet long and twelve feet wide, would in time, we felt sure, make a fine support for the vines, a good background for the hardy border, and link the wild woods with the smooth expanse of lawn. Paved with brick, laid herring-bone fashion in sand, it became a favorite walk on dewy mornings.

Company in plenty was always there. In early Spring the robins were busy with their nests and broods overhead, yellow warblers flitted in and out of the climbing roses, the grosbeak and his little brown mate sought a building-site, and a pair of thrushes were sure to float down to the hollow boulder near, for their daily splash. All summer long, gray squirrels ran over the loosely-laid rafters, and chipmunks rustled in the leaves, to appear before one, and squeal for the accustomed nut. In the early Fall the Louisiana water thrush teetered under the salvia blossoms, and chickadees called merrily from the tall dry sunflowers in the woods close by. The yellow leaves came tumbling down, the bending oak was crimson against the sky, and we said, "Can any season be more beautiful than Fall?"

In winter, under the snow, the pergola was still more picturesque. Blue shadows lay on the glistening ground, and every cranny and tiny crack was filled with soft white powdery flakes. The oak leaves rustled in the sharp air, the sky was all a wonderful blue, the trunks of the trees were velvety black, and every blade and leaf and twig was glistening with ice in the sunshine.

But, after all, midsummer finds it in its glory. All about the posts are twined the wild virgin's bower, with its cousin from Japan, a little clematis Jackmanni and the pure white Henryi; the woodbine of course, and the wild grape, the akebia quinata and the rampant kudzu vine; the old-fashioned Prairie Queen rose and the Baltimore Belle and the crimson rambler in splendid great sprays of bloom twenty feet long; plenty of eglantine, delicious under the hot sun, the northern fox and the Niagara grape and that splendid climber, the trumpet-vine.

At one end, by the house, is a small terra cotta wall-fountain from Florence, and a convenient bench; at the other the pergola broadens into a square tea-house with old wooden seats in the corners, a stump for a table, and in the centre a spikenard from the woods, growing in one of Nature's *jardinières.*

To the north a narrow path leads from this end of the pergola, under the lindens and maples, to the kitchen garden not far away; while on the west another path lined with meadow-rue, columbine, and the spikenard, connects with the service road and cottage and upper garden.

On the woodsy side of the pergola grow the golden glow, and plumed poppy, the tall Eulalia grass, and the plumed ravenna reed, which my grandmother used to call ribbon grass. Here are the scarlet balm and wild sunflowers and ferns and brakes of every variety, and wild lilies where they like, the old wood lily and the yellow Canada, the Turk's cap, and the Carolina, the Grayi and the Elegans. Nearer the house are the bane-berries, both red and white, the ginseng and columbine and Jack-in-the-pulpit, mixed with violets and hepaticas and asters and golden rod, all blending imperceptibly into the underbrush of the thick woods.

On this side extends the laundry-yard wall. What a time I had trying to find a spot wherein to dry the clothes! It must be in the bright sun and yet hidden in a corner; it must be close to the house yet not visible from it. In our dilemma one daring soul ventured to suggest a steam drying machine! In the country! On a seventy-two-acre lot! No, I scorned such a solution; with the Constant Improver's fertile brain, I knew in time the right place would be found, and found it was. All housekeepers will appreciate my satisfaction when I was given a grassy space flooded with the southwest sun and enclosed on the east and north by a wall six feet high. The English

have learned the beauty that lies in long surfaces of wall, and do not hesitate, even in small estates, thus to enclose the space necessaryfor working purposes. This rough plaster wall, extending from the kitchen-house some fifty feet to the north and topped by heavy brown timber, had at its southern end a dear old-fashioned latched door of rough brown planks, bound together with long iron hasps. On either side of the door were inserted bits of plaster heads and the whole wall was soon draped in the prolific folds of the kudzu vine. The grassy yard was so bare, so clean, so practical! What was my astonishment to discover one morning a thrifty rose vine, climbing vigorously up in the corner! Now roses are one of my treasures, but not in my laundry yard, as thorns and clothes and wind are not a felicitous combination. I protested, but the Constant Improver said it was such a sunny corner, he didn't believe the clothes would get torn. Wouldn't I let it stay for a month and see? This sounded reasonable enough, and I gave orders that his clothes should be hung nearest that sunniest corner. The rose grew and flourished, it put forth great bunches of sweet blossoms, it also sent out long stalks; but the Constant Improver as usual was right, and no damage was done. So now we have a whole row of roses on the south side of the laundry wall, and the effect is charming.

On the east side of the pergola lies the hardy border, in irregular outline. The lawn creeps up to the edge of the brick walk temptingly in two or three places as if to say, "Come try my yielding turf; let your foot sink into the clover deep; come hunt for the mushroom's fairy ring, and see for yourself how the violet blows."

Every three years the hardy border is trenched two feet down, fertilized and replanted, the peonies only are not disturbed, nor the vines, of course, nor the old-fashioned yellow roses. On the outer edge along its entire length the yellow jonquils blossom in the early Spring. Under the bending oak and straight young maple tree, where the vines did not get enough light to cover well the posts, we put a high-bush cranberry and a Sieboldei polygonum, supposed to be a dwarf, but it turned out to be a verb instead of a noun, and dwarfed everything within reach of its roots.

This border is an everlasting topic of discussion. Every year we try something new; it is so tempting an experimental station. Do the results ever equal the highly colored prints in the seed catalogues? Much less would satisfy us. With a space over two hundred feet long and from four to six feet wide there certainly should be room for everything. But we like great masses of color. Twenty feet of cherry phlox against as many Shasta daisies; quantities of Sweet Williams and pyrethrums; a big patch of columbines with their varied blooms and finely cut foliage, the old-fashioned favorite, with the pale yellow variety, and the exquisite blue, sent to us by a friend from Colorado. It was quite a revelation to us to find seven different species of columbines, thus prolonging their season from May to September. Gradually they seem to have been trained to lift their modest heads until one pure white variety frankly looks up at the sunshine and is not afraid. One July morning I counted one hundred and sixteen Madonna lilies rising from the peony clumps, and later the Japanese golden-banded variety took their places.

All hardy borders should have plenty of white and yellow flowers; they blend with everything else and separate any clashing colors. The scarlet of the Oriental poppies, the lychnis, and the salvia need careful management. They should have a far corner to themselves, in the midst of fine greenery. Along the brick walk the star of Bethlehem opens to the early sunshine, and the Virginia waterleaf lifts her cups of nectar to the knowing bees.

At the farther end of the border were some curious flat mullein-like rosettes which I watched all one summer, but nothing happened. The rain and heavy dew rested in great globules on their thick hairy leaves, the sun shone as encouragingly upon them as on the blossoms of the yellow chamomile close by, but it was not until the following year that my patience was rewarded. In a night, apparently, a tall spray some two to three feet high suddenly shot from the middle of each rough rosette, bearing graceful rows of curious long-lipped creamy flowers, and the battle of the bees began. This white salvia is most amusing, — such masking of batteries, such bombarding of pollen; and, at the close, both parties are victorious.

How many blue flowers we find in this hardy border! The Greek valerian, sent by a dear friend from the White Mountains, has taken kindly to its new home, and in the middle of May fifty great clusters of delicate blossoms greeted us at once. The whole tribe of larkspur is a delight. To our surprise even the annuals sowed themselves this year under the sweet-brier bushes and put forth great stalks of pure pink the exact tone of the roses above. They grow also in deep purple and pale lavender and greenish white; while the perennials in immense long spikes of indescribable pinks and blues, and pure blues, and blue-and-purples, blossomed gayly twice during the season. The Chinese is perhaps my favorite, the color is so pure and it lasts for days. The Canterbury bells are another joyous family, from the baby harebells faintly tinkling in the grass to the ten-foot stalks of the pyramidal, blue and white and gaudy. The rampion in the herb garden is a humble relative, and the Chinese bellflowers both blue and white, single and double, carry on the family characteristics. The veronica too is a most exquisite shade either in the tall or dwarf species, and keeps green after even ten degrees of frost.

Fortunately we are allowed to cut flowers from the hardy border, and the Constant Improver looks most picturesque, though quite unconscious, as he saunters down the shadowy walk laden with great stalks of blazing star, or leopard's bane, or the obedient plant whose blossoms stay whichever side of the stalk the wind or the mischievous boy may place them.

The pergola is a favorite racing stretch for our boy visitors. One, two, three, and away from the stone bench to the goal, — the stump at the farther end. The young girls in white frocks, their arms about each other's waist, exchange confidences, as they stroll demurely back and forth; the shadows from the vine-hung rafters touch them gently as they pass. Even our "most grave and reverend seigneurs" I find pacing up and down the moss-edged walk, drinking in the fragrant air of early morning. Sometimes they are nature-loving "seigneurs" and come in with bunches of "yellow daises," as they call the lance-leaved coreopsis which apparently grows wild in every spare corner, the whole length of the hardy border.

Down through the pergola comes every morning the kitchen-gardener laden with his baskets of freshly gathered fruits and veg-

etables. If the children are near, they rush to meet him begging a few strawberries or raspberries for their doll's tea-party on the stone bench under the Florentine fountain. Every one knows how hungry dolls get about the middle of the morning, and here are food and drink in one. Such an opportunity must not be neglected!

The only thing which one very conventional lady could find to admire about our place was the smooth acre of turf which lay at the back of the house and was bounded by the hardy border of the pergola on the west, and the woods on the other two sides, making the foil, the contrasting element to all our wildness.

Not but what we had pleasures and pictures on the lawn too. Could anything be more graceful than the squirrel's leap or the sweeping flash of the tanager? In early Fall the marigolds and salvia, filling in all bare spaces along the hardy border, are a favorite field for the humming-birds, and the New England asters' rich purple attracts the white butterflies by the hundred. With what keen pleasure we watch the rhythmic swing of the long rake as it gathers into heaps the freshly mown grass, or the slow moving of the low latticed leaf-cart on its broad tires!

After a rain in October, indeed during it, if possible, the sower with his big bag of grass seed under his arm appears at the end of the pergola and, stepping onto the lawn, slowly crosses it, back and forth, throwing in graceful curves the clouds of fine grass seed, hunting out the brown spots where the dandelions have flourished and carefully avoiding the mushrooms cropping out in all sorts of unexpected places. Finally the bag is empty, turned inside out with a parting shake, and the old sou'wester and slouch hat disappear slowly down the winding path, in search of further work.

Somehow, few of our guests seem to feel its importance when I announce the great events happening in our daily existence. For instance, when I exclaim, "The small thrushes in the long-path nest sailed out into the world to-day," or "There are ninety-three blossoms on that one spray of crimson ramblers over the south terrace wall," or "The first monkshood opened this morning," our visitors politely answer: "Indeed!" but I can feel their thoughts are wandering. Only a few really enter into our inner joyous eventful life, where each day brings forth a revelation and a miracle.

A
LITTLE
MARYLAND
GARDEN

by

Helen Ashe Hays

1 9 0 9

WHOEVER HAS A GARDEN has a perennial source of interest, whether the garden itself be large or small. Indeed, though the large garden has wide spaces and beautiful vistas, the owner of the small one has the pleasure of being personally acquainted with every plant and shrub in it. And if the owner be a woman, the small garden gives her perhaps the more pleasure because she can work in it, spade, plant, and prune it herself, and know that the result is all the work of her own hands.

My little garden seems wonderfully interesting because I have done everything for it. I can see it as it was — a clay waste, generally muddy and hopeless-looking. It lies behind a half-timbered cottage, and is enclosed by a high wall, so that from the first it had the advantage of privacy. I was told when I came into the house that a good motto for it would be one seen carved on a cottage in the Bavarian Alps, "Klein aber Mein." Since I have become a gardener I have often thought its homely content just expressed my feeling for the little garden behind it.

For some time after I came into possession, the house had first to be considered, and spending on the garden was a luxury. Some one has said that none but the poor know how good the poor are to each other; and surely none but garden lovers know how generous their fellow gardeners can be. Just when I had seriously determined that I must, at all costs, make my plot of ground into a garden, I was given a number of shrubs that were lifted from an old place in the town. There were deutzias and weigelias, a dozen large bushes of the "Rose of Sharon" (altheas), two fine Japan quinces, a white currant, and some old-fashioned hundred-leaf roses. Also, to my great delight, there were two lilac bushes. Lilacs would not bloom in the part of California where my life up to this time had been spent, and they seemed to me delightfully characteristic of the East, making one think of old homesteads and early settlers. Their heavy, languorous perfume seems to typify the exuberant rush of life of an Eastern spring. I looked forward to gathering great armfuls of my own lilac blooms, but so far they have been something of a disappointment, refusing to do anything more than grow. I have since had presents of lilacs from two other gardens, and though all take kindly to their new quarters I have gathered only one vaseful of purple blooms. Last year I sent to a florist for two French varieties,

"La Tour d'Auvergne" and "Marie Legraye," and hope in time to have a quantity of these lovely flowers.

Soon after two other shrubs were added to my collection, a fragrant old-fashioned mock-orange, and a Forsythia *suspensa,* which blooms in early spring before the leaves come out, and becomes a mass of gold from the ground to the highest twig.

After the shrubs came a present from a maiden lady whose garden is said to be the trimmest in town. She sent me tulips and iris roots. Another friend contributed some feverfew plants, whose descendants are still ready to step into the breach and grow anywhere I put them, filling up any odd corner with their pretty foliage and white flower heads. I never saw such useful bloomers and willing garden hacks. Another gift was made of orange lilies and white chrysanthemums.

Here was indeed a start for a little garden. Only the tulips failed to adapt themselves to their new position. The iris increased so that last year I gave away a wheelbarrowful of roots, and never missed them. The feverfew, which seeds itself, is contantly being pulled up and thrown over the fence, put in temporarily to fill up a bed till something else is ready to go into it, transplanted, and generally used and abused; and still thrusts itself forward with perfect good humour, seeming to say, "Here I am, make use of me." It emerges from the snows of winter with some of its vivid green in fairly good order, and all summer its soft tufts of white are interposed between highly coloured neighbours, that might swear at each other but for its harmonising influence.

But to go back to the beginning, the clay waste must be made into a garden. It was cut through the middle of its length by a brick walk, and I had but one idea in the start, to sow it in grass, and not cut the lawn up into flower beds. I had never heard of William Robinson, and Wilkinson Elliott was a stranger to me. It was, therefore, instinct that led me to keep my flowers back in borders rather than cut up the lawn with circles and ovals. And it was necessity that guided me in the choice of hardy plants to fill the borders. I was away from the house all day, except for an occasional holiday, so I must choose what would thrive with the smallest amount of attention. I wanted to put into the ground what would stay there and grow willingly, without having to be renewed or brought in during the winter months. I read catalogues and studied perennials and annuals. I took no interest in biennials. Plants that kept one waiting for flowers for a whole year, and after blooming for one season died, were not for a beginner. One most important feature of gardening I did not appreciate at all in the beginning, the matter of soil and manure.

My first attempt at making borders was in the L that ran up beside the house and was overlooked by the porch and the dining-room windows. It was small, sheltered, and private; a little nook that might be made gay with flowers. Unfortunately the soil was a filling of brickbats and builders' rubbish, and in my haste to begin I only put a layer of proper soil on top. But I had beginners' luck. Under the grey stone foundation wall of the house I planted German iris, and in the opposite border sweet-williams and mignonette. Both did well, and the descendants of the sweet-williams have never deteriorated, but are as handsome and thriving to-day as in the start. They range through every shade of pink and red to deep crimson. Some are pure white, and others white marked with crimson or purple eyes. I pick them by armfuls, with stems two feet long. They seed themselves and supply any vacant place where they may be wanted in the garden, and I divide them in the fall.

By degrees, I added other flowers to this bed. Hollyhocks now range tall and stately against the wall, and there are tall plants of perennial phlox between them and the sweet-williams. This arrangement is broken at intervals by Anthony Waterer spireas (which by the way I think are very much overrated), spirea *palmata*, a clump of Japanese anemones and *candidum* lilies. A white fraxinella is at one end, and halfway down, the silvery foliage of a bush of "Old Man" makes a soft background for the flower tints before it.

Almost all of these additions were raised from tiny plants sold by a neighbouring florist in the summer for very low prices. This nurseryman sends out lists of shrubs and plants every season, and if one has the patience to watch over the little plants, and protect them from the summer's heat, many additions can be made to the garden, that would soon exhaust one's purse if they were bought at the  regular prices. There is, of course, some risk, as the weather is so unfavourable, and it takes a good deal of determination to begin raising a shrub when its size is almost microscopic. But from these small beginnings I have brought up some fine wistarias and climbing roses, spireas, both "Anthony Waterer" and Reevsii, as well as the handsome herbaceous *palmata,* and am now trying to induce a laburnum to do credit to my powers as a gardener.

This laburnum was so tiny when it came that I carried it over the first winter in the house, and in the spring sunk the pot in the border, where it was forgotten. It was entirely neglected until one day in the fall. I was having a fall cleaning in the borders, energetically pulling up and cutting back, when I came upon it, a little worse for the indefatigable summer insects but really wanting to grow. I decided to take the chances of its being able to stand the winter in the open, and planted it out permanently. It was enriched with cow manure and protected with coarse litter, and is now adding cubits to its stature in a very satisfactory way.

I have just come across one of the old lists I sent, which included perennial asters, sweet rocket, valerian and wallflower, Shasta daisy and plume pink, and other border plants. I remember the valerian was chosen for sentiment. One of my most vivid flower memories is of the Mission Dolores in San Francisco, on a May day. The sky was of the deepest blue, the air golden with sunshine, and the graveyard beside the Mission was one mass of climbing roses, arching over everything, flinging masses of bloom everywhere, lavish as only California roses can be. And beneath them a deeper note of pink struck by the valerian that grew everywhere among and over the graves, holding up soft pink tufts to the sun. Both were so exuberant, so full of life over the grey headstones. I think every county in Ireland was commemorated on these stones, from County Cork to County Tyrone. And, sharing this "garden of sleep" with them in equal numbers, one read the liquid names of Spain, Vincente and Orestes, Soledad and Ramona. I have never forgotten the impression made by this joyous, flowery burying place, so I got some pink valerian in memory of the Mission Dolores.

Wallflowers I know were chosen to try to add to my stock, for I have had my sorrows by reason of wallflowers. In California they grow wild, and in a garden where I once lived there was a long row of them under the pepper trees. One February I sowed seed in the house of perennial wallflowers, raised a number of little plants, set them out, and carried at least a dozen through a severe winter; read that bone meal was their favourite spring tonic, and sent for a package of bone meal. I had something brought to me with the message that the dealer "was out of bone meal, but this was a fertiliser, and splendid for flowers, and would do just as well." So I stirred it about their roots to make them comfortable and happy, and they promptly, all but one, "up and died." I killed quite a number of other plants with that fertiliser, but I mourned for none of them as I did for my wallflowers. One survived, and brought out handsome double flowers, fragrant, and in those iron-rust tones that wallflowers usually have. The little wallflowers from the florist did not survive the move in the summer heat, so this old veteran still holds the fort, huddled close to the stone wall. These plants seem to need the proximity of stone, just as fig-trees need human companionship, to make them thrive. Fig-trees will flourish beside a home, even if neglected. But let human beings leave them, and they soon pine and die.

I recollect having a special mission for the Shasta daisy, which was to put it between some orange lilies on the one hand, and a group of pink and crimson phlox on the other. I thought a great white daisy bush would make a break between these pronounced colours. The florist reserves the right to substitute in case he is short, and my disgust can be imagined when I found that he had substituted an English daisy for my order. The "wee, modest" flower could not fill the position, nor even "rattle round in it," as Holmes once said.

My second border was made across the back of the house wall, and filled with daffodils. In my old home we had no daffodils, and when I came to Maryland I fell in love with them. It is quite impossible to express the feeling of pleasure they give in the spring. They are so hardy and dauntless, coming with the first hint of mild weather, braving winds and frost with their grace and dainty colouring. My favourites are the long trumpets, and among these I like best those with yellow trumpet and white perianth. But broad-faced Sir Watkin is delightful for his robust, hearty look, and orange phoenix, with its full heads spilling apart to show a touch of orange, is a beautiful cut flower. I add to my stock every year some new varieties, and put them not only in the borders, but in unoccupied nooks and corners of the garden. I must have them in quantities, both to nod in the spring breezes and to cut for the house. I have now the following sorts:

Empress	Von Sion	Grandee
Emperor	Mrs. Langtry	Poeticus
Horsfieldii	Leedsii	Poeticus Ornatus
Orange Phoenix	Stella	Princeps Maximus.

They are all lovely. The only failure I have had was the *alba plena odorata,* and I was warned beforehand that it rarely bloomed in this country.

I have been criticised for speaking of the long trumpet varieties as daffodils, instead of calling them narcissus. Some people have a passion for being correct, but the name of daffodil is endeared to us by poetry. We hear March called "the roaring moon of daffodil and crocus," and read of the "host of golden daffodils." Their praises are sung by all our old English favourites. Bailey tells us that the distinction is only made in this country, and that in England the term narcissus is only applied to the *poeticus*.

It was from such small beginnings that my garden took shape, and the time soon came when I was able to divide and multiply, to stock new borders, and even send plants out into the marsh. Among the plants that increased rapidly were the orange lilies and certain bluebells that were given me. The giver had forgotten just what they were, but they answered to the description given in catalogues of campanula *persicifolia*. They throw up long spikes of flowers of a dainty lavender-blue, and spread so fast that they remind me of the remark of a California acquaintance about her eucalyptus tree, that "it was the most profligate tree she ever saw." They bloom for a long time if the old flowers are cut off, and make a good mass of cool colour. From these two plants I made an orange and blue border, where there had been a troublesome strip of grass. It was between the brick path leading from the side gate to the back of the house, and the garden wall, and was just too narrow to be mown, and just too wide to cut well with the shears, and so it often looked ragged and untidy. But spaded up and planted thickly with lilies at the back, bordered with the bluebells, it made an effective strip of colour, and only asked to be let alone.

The lawn grass made the upper part of the garden an even green, but in the lower part the dandelions disputed every inch of ground with it. They look so beautiful, starring the grass with gold, that the first year they had things rather their own way. It needs time, and a sense of having been taken advantage of, to steel our hearts against anything so fine as dandelions. They take the garden by storm with their shining stars, but they come to be "a glistering grief," "a golden sorrow." They call out one of the most fertile garden crops — moral reflections. I defy any one to turn gardener and not fall a-moralising like a parson. Given a March morning, a windy blue sky, white fleecy clouds blown past, the mountains like a distant wall, Mr. Robin strutting on the lawn, proud as if he had brought it all to pass; and the grass a mass of winking suns. What a strong moral sense pervades one's being as he digs up and casts away these alluring weeds! What beautiful maxims form spontaneously in his mind! And what a comfort it is to feel that he is out in the soft spring wind and sunshine, not from self-indulgence, but accomplishing a duty!

As I write the snow lies on the ground, patchily, not with a good warm covering, but like a tattered shawl that lets in the cold. I know just where to look for the newcomers in the borders when spring calls them out. I have put out some crown imperials, flowers that I have read of but never seen. I have planted both English cottage tulips, and the late Darwins, and some little sweet-scented Florentines. I love these jewels of colour in the spring. I have put out, also, dozens of Roman hyacinths, blue, red, and blush, because I have seen a garden which has wreaths of them about the flower beds. And I know that with the coming of spring my flowering shrubs will spread their white and pink plumes, sweet-williams and daffodils will paint the borders with a bold brush, orange lilies bloom beside fragrant June roses. For my little garden is fairly started now. I have gone on adding new borders when I had time to work, getting in supplies of street sweepings and manure and leaf mould. And these new borders have been filled with occasional purchases of plants, and with such hardy perennials as an amateur can raise from seed. Above all, digging, bordering, planting, everything almost without exception had been done with my own hands. And this is the greatest pleasure to be had from gardening after all, to be close to the warm earth, indifferent to clothes, watching the tiny forms of life, and happily at work.

THE
FIRST
YEAR

---

by
Hanna Rion

1912

ONCE UPON A TIME two people, who were very world-fagged, came to their senses and realized that the cure for their mind sickness lay beyond the clank of business chains, the sight of sky-scrapers and the whir of elevated trains.

Their apparent quarrel with life was really only hunger for the song of wild birds, the nearness of great fields of pasture, the friendship of hills, the sight of a brook breaking ice barriers in spring, the artillery of forest limbs snapping in icy grip, the lowing of cattle at eventide, the elbow touch with simple, kindly folk, and above all to own a slice of this great birthday cake of earth.

When you buy a piece of land, remember — you own all above it; you own that far reach of ether in which the stars drift over your land, the moon as it hangs above your trees, the sun as it passes through your sky-claim; and best of all you possess all the dreams which lie between you and infinity.

And you own down, down, down to the centre of the earth's axis, and this is why owning land gives one such a sense of anchorage and solidity.

When we came to our senses (for my humbler half and I are the people of whom I spoke so mysteriously in my opening sentence) we sought the country and became the proud possessors of a slice of land and a real home. On our original plot — before we bought the adjoining two acres of wilderness — there stood two apple trees, three peaches, two cherries, white and purple lilacs, a deutzia, and a flowering almond, — nothing else. Now, after a few years, to tell all our tree and flower possessions would necessitate nine volumes of very fine print, and then I'd have to leave out all the intangible things we have come to own, things which have no name but which make one terribly happy in the private possession thereof.

The first autumn we spent so much time in congratulating each other on our emancipation from the city, marveling at the sunsets, rediscovering the night sky, that we were really too stunned by the seventy and seven wonders of the world revealed each day to think about gardening. So it was not until we had had a whole winter in which to catch our breath, that we even discussed flowers. When I look back on that time I find we really didn't know the ABC's of gardening (though we both thought ourselves very wise), and that is why we've had such a joyful, growing time of it, blundering along, learning bit by bit through a hundred mistakes; and even after all these years we know there are equally many surprises ahead and that six years hence, today will be called blind and ignorant.

When the thought of garden dawned we began very modestly, thinking of attempting only the easiest, simplest things. When we pored over the catalogues, we paused only at the familiar names and the ones we could pronounce; we both shied dreadfully at botanical titles.

Then in our spring rambles of discovery we came across many deserted farms and gaunt, ghostly houses with weed-choked gardens. With fine moral scruples we rescued many plants which would otherwise have died of neglect, pining for human love. Of course some people might call this procedure hard names, but it depends wholly on the point of view. I'm sure it's a very fine kind of missionary work to relieve an old forgotten hollyhock of its poor little children who are being choked to death by weeds and haven't a chance in the world. Then, too, a scraggly old lilac will be very grateful if you help yourself to the dozens of suckers which are needlessly draining its health.

It was by means of such salvage that we started a lilac hedge and were blessed by a row of blooming hollyhocks from the piazza to the road, the summer after their rescue.

There is no shorter route to country neighbors' hearts than a love of flowers. Country people are not specialists, carefully guarding rare flower treasures; they are, on the contrary, big-hearted owners of nice old-fashioned plants which they got through earlier neighbors' giving, and which they in turn pass on to flower-loving newcomers.

So it happened I soon found each call from a neighbor meant the enriching of our garden by iris, rockets or hardy phlox clumps, while a return call meant being the recipient of dozens of slips and roots. I never before found it so easy and pleasant to remember my social duties.

The really permanent things which found place in our garden the first spring were therefore gotten either by loot or by gift; the remaining plants were annuals, and wild things borrowed from fields, woods and swamps.

For the sake of other beginners who want to do the thing gradually and make a modest beginning in gardening, I can't do better than tell them of our annuals that first season, and how much beauty we surrounded ourselves with by sowing only the best-known seed.

To start with, we found an old chicken yard on the place; and as we couldn't undertake chickens we removed the chicken houses and stored the lumber for the making of toolhouse and hotbed the following spring, reserving one long stretch of the chicken wire for the support of sweet peas.

The rich soil of the former fowl yard made an ideal place to start our seedbeds, and here we sowed in May, blue *ageratum*, Marguerite carnations, cosmos, asters, marigolds, mignonette and pansies. We planted at each column of the front porch wild clematis found in a brush tangle near a brookside. The clematis is a long-legged vine which remains as bare about the knees as a Highlander, so we planted nasturtiums to cover the lower part of these vines; and sweet alyssum plants were invited to do the same favor for the nasturtiums, as they grew tall and given to yellow leaves about the feet.

From the porch to the road the aforesaid hollyhocks were permitted to fulfill their prim mission by being placed in a straight row next to the walk. At their backs, adjoining the lawn, we placed alternate clumps of gift iris and hardy phlox, with a generous sowing of opium poppies to insure midsummer gayety. Then we removed the few lonesome and purposeless shrubs dotted about the lawn to the other boundary of our grass plot, and by leaving an unbroken lawn we greatly improved the appearance of our frontage. To surround these shrubs and to keep them from feeling hurt, we made a long irregular bed, which ran between an apple and a cherry tree, holding a very indiscriminate lot of plants and a perfect kaleidoscope of color; we had not grown fastidious then and we wanted *flowers*, no matter whether they were intended for bedfellows or not.

Here California poppies, marigolds and *calliopsis* made a blaze of gold; cornflowers, larkspurs and *ageratum* equaled the sky in blueness; and *Phlox Drummondi* of every shade of salmon pink, white and red, were rivaled by the motley colors of the variegated pansy border. It was beautiful chaos, and taught us much of the extent to which nature can combine colors without jarring the eye.

At the rear we transformed a spinster-looking outbuilding by draping its straight front with morning glories, cunningly lured by strings tacked to the very pinnacle of the roof. On the other side of the building, in the shade, we planted in our blissful ignorance a long row of sunflowers; in effort to see their god, the sun, they were forced to grow to an unheard-of height, their shining faces smiling fully sixteen feet from the ground.

Bordering the path leading to the seed yard, we made a hedge of four-o'clocks. In a long bed at the side of the back yard were planted candytuft, *dianthus,* Marguerite carnations, asters and cosmos. Well, you should have seen the bloom and riot of color in the midst of which we had our happy being that season! It began with the May snowdrift of candytuft, and lasted through the midsummer blare of marigolds, larkspur and poppies to the asters in early fall, and the tall cosmos which bloomed long into October, as the frost was late that year.

We had no problems at that time; there were no roses to spray and carry over winter, no perennials to mulch in the fall, — just a season of irresponsible joy, color and fragrance, with nothing to do but eradicate weeds and pick flowers. But, being human, we were not content; we had drunk of the wine of lure, and we secretly conspired to add to our problems next season by entering further into the land of flowers, and acquiring an adjoining wilderness of two and a half acres to hold all our planned-for treasures.

All winter long we pored over new catalogues, mouthing the strange names of biennials and perennials, the married and single names of roses, and the hieroglyphic-like titles of lilies.

From a modest beginning that first year we have become flower gourmands and experimentalists, just as you, too, are sure to be, once you enter the boundaries of that realm whose enchantments know no limitations.

RETROSPECT AND PROSPECT

by

J. Horace McFarland

1915

L OOKING BACKWARD, I note the transition
from reading books about gardens to doing
work in one of them, and how it gradually came
to pass that I read less, and only of standard substan-
tialities that might be termed principles, because I found
that I must work out my own garden salvation, and

work it out, if not with fear and trembling, certainly with an open mind and a humble disposition. If I may be pardoned the personality of it, I may say, too, that the garden-work stopped a rather busy pen for a while. How could I take time to write of anything — gardening or printing, civics or photography — when there was such an open volume to read as I walked and worked and thought? Of this kind of reading I have done much, and profited by it some at least, in these garden years. Now that something has moved me to write again, I am but talking with whoever reads, feeling hopeful that those who have followed the fortunes of this growing garden along through the months have arrived at some sympathy with and understanding of my plain statement of happenings and hopes, of errors and satisfactions.

In this retrospect, I observe that much has been done at Breeze Hill, from the standpoint of the gardenerless garden and the scanty pocketbook, though it would be little indeed in comparison with what many men of large means have accomplished in less time. Such men's gardens interest me to look at, and in part to profit by; but I take it more men of little means who ought to make grow a garden of their own will see these words than will millionaires whose very weight of wealth makes an individual garden almost impossible for them. So my measure of accomplishment in working over this run-down old place is only to be considered in connection with the expenditure of time and money possible to many another man who will be made a better worker at his business or profession if he will undertake the garden cure.

There has been a heavy snow, and I write looking west through Lovers' Lane, where I see the planting of rhododendrons along the old-looking but quite recent stone walk that has taken the place of the weedy, rutty farm lane of five years ago. The rhododendrons, snow-bound as they are, look happy, and are happy; and I know that at their feet and along the walk on both sides are safely tucked away scores of woods favorites in this place reserved for American natives only. Just around to the right there is, I also know, a planting of daffodils that will surely look better than did the poke-weed that overran the same place five years ago. To the right also, and following the line of the old hedge that has been petted and trimmed and fertilized all I dare, more and other daffodils will come, and later Easter lilies and later yet fine little yellow button chrysanthemums, where reigned supreme dock and nettles in the old days.

Looking southwest, I see the youngest part of the garden, with its borders and the Arboretum bed, its grass driveway, its almost concealed range of coldframes facing the winter sun, its new planting of pet evergreens. That was a wreck of dead pear trees five years ago! Beyond, I see the barberry hedge, now purely lovely because of the way in which it carries its snow load, and I remember that when I came here there were fences that were offenses — great scroll-sawed contortions of pine boards — because they said plainly, "Stay out!" This hedge, which is only a marking line, after all, says "Look in!"

Walking out in the snow — and I love it more than I did that first winter — I turn into the formal garden which has taken the place of two broken-down buildings — an ice-house and a greenhouse — that made the place forlorn when I came. In it I see the rose-arbor, now trebly covered with a mat of prosperous rose-twigs, snugly protected with the unused Christmas trees I have picked up, and thick with this clinging snow. Under these nearby flat white expanses I know there are perennial plants of many sorts, ready to be born again in spring; and they grow in what was formerly the foundation of that greenhouse.

A bit farther along, and there is a glimpse of the fruit-garden, looking clean and trim, and also ready to serve me beyond my deserts when its time comes. And this has taken the place of an abandoned, overrun, ridgy, dying vineyard of five years ago!

All this change; and yet it is, and looks like, an old place. Not only had I a memory of my own old home place to restrain me, but I had the admonitions of Mr. Manning, to prevent the sort of horror I have so often seen with sadness — the cutting down of everything, so as to "start afresh." Here, instead, the old features have been zealously preserved, and the new plantings and placings adapted to them. The result is a mature and home-ly (please note the hyphen, and what it means) beauty that could not have been had in a generation if we had "started afresh."

The retrospect is pleasing, at least to us of the growing garden, in and with which we also have grown and gained in spirit and in health. Now what of the prospect?

These vista plant-pictures are to be perfected, so that they will tell us in every season more of the goodness of the God of the outdoors. This implies study, effort, fruitful mistakes, trials, changes. Then I want here gathered, not in a museum fashion of orderly display, but as part of a living and growing garden, all the good plants, particularly of Pennsylvania, that can be happily located. I want also the less well-known shrubs, especially of fascinating West China and mysterious Thibet, to show here to visiting Americans what they may additionally have of loveliness in leaf and flower. I want good fruits — I have already supplemented those fine fall-bearing Progressive strawberries with a red raspberry said to come along in company — and new roses that are worth while.

The vegetable part of the garden I hope to see take cognizance of other things that we ought to like, and to repeat many times the success of the kohlrabi. I hope constantly to improve the texture and the productivity of the soil. I want to some time have really good lawns — for it may have been noticed that I have kept quiet about lawns, for reasons, many reasons — and I dream of grass drives as deep and velvety and wear-resisting as those of my old acquaintance Olcott in Connecticut.

And I must not forget my dream of a little well-placed rock-garden, in which may be made at home a host of lovely plants that demand cool roots, and a chance to nestle under the edge of a boulder. There is a place for it, I think; and also a place for just a bit of a water garden, well circumstanced, in which I may see bloom the lovely hardy water lilies, and around which may be gathered some wet-footed plants.

There are two old cherry trees in the front lawn that are dying. At the foot of the most decrepit is growing an Excelsa rose, which in one season has mounted about fifteen feet and ought in due course to swing its crimson garlands in the breeze from the topmost remaining limbs another year. This is the trial; and if it seems a success, the other old veteran will change its bearing in June from cherries to roses, or mayhap wistaria.

Other things are to be done. The good plants I want to naturalize as "weeds" are to be selected and placed; the iris planting is to be made more representative; a peony garden will come if "shekels" appear for it; some North Carolina mountain evergreen shrubs — the leucothoë, the galax, and certain azalea-rhododendrons — are to fill a corner that will be home for them, I hope; a long hedge of climbers, not roses, is to form a semi-screen for the west garden. Thus, and otherwise, the garden is to grow; for it is, and has been, a true growing garden. And I have thought it worth while, in planning and planting, to take into account what would happen if again this old place were abandoned. God willing, I believe that even then it would continue to be a growing garden. I should like no better epitaph than that it might be said, after I have passed along to other labors, that here dwelt a man who loved a garden, who lived in and grew with it, and who yet looks upon it, even from afar, as a garden growing for all who love the beauties of God's green earth.

BALANCE
IN
THE
FLOWER
GARDEN

---

by

Mrs. Francis King

1915

W HEN THE CHANCE to arrange the
planting of a formal garden of my
own fell into my hands, about eight years
ago, I felt strongly the need of advice in what I
was about to do. Advice, however, was not forthcom-

ing, and at the outset I fell, of course, into the pit of absurdity. Without any reason for so doing, I decided to arrange the planting in this garden (a balanced design in four equal parts with eight beds in each section) as though the whole were a scrap of perennial border a few feet wide and a few feet long. The ridiculous idea occurred to me to have the garden a picture to be looked at from the house alone. The matter of garden design was to fade out of sight except with regard to the few beds immediately surrounding the small central pool. These were planted more or less formally, with heliotrope in the four parallelograms nearest the centre, and iris and lilies in four other spaces near the rest. I endeavored to produce irregular crosswise banks of color from the far end of the garden to the part nearest the house — scarlet, orange, and yellow, with a fair sprinkling of hollyhocks in yellow and white on the more distant edge; before these, crowds of white flowers, gray-leaved plants and blue-flowering things; and, nearest of all to the beholder, brighter and paler pinks.

The result was nothing but an ugly muddle — indescribably so when one happened to be in the midst of the garden itself. For two or three years I bore with this unhappy condition of things; indeed, nothing but the fact that the flowers conducted themselves in remarkably luxuriant and brilliant fashion, due to the freshness and richness of the soil, could have saved me from seeing sooner the silly mistake I had made; when, chancing to look down upon the garden from an upper window, the real state of things suddenly revealed itself, and from that day I set about to plan and plant in totally different fashion.

With Mr. Robinson, I feel against the wretched carpet-bedding system, while I quite agree, on the other hand, with the spokesman for the formalists, Reginald Blomfield, who declared that there is no such thing as the "wild garden," that the name is a contradiction of terms. The one thing I do maintain is that advice, the very best advice, is the prime necessity: for those who can afford it, the fine landscape architect; for those who cannot, the criticism or counsel of some friend or acquaintance whose experience has been wider than their own. The time is sure to come when experts in the art of proper flower-grouping alone will be in demand.

There is no doubt about it, our grandmothers were right when they preferred to see a vase on each side of the clock! With a given length of shelf and a central object on that shelf, one's instinct for equalizing calls for a second candlestick or bowl to balance the first. My meaning may be illustrated by a recent picture in "The Century Magazine" of Mrs. Tyson's beautiful garden at Berwick, Maine. Charming as is this lovely garden-vista, with its delightful posts in the foreground, repeating the lines of slim poplar in the middle distance, it would have given me much more pleasure could those heavy-headed white or pale-colored phloxes on the right have had a perfect repetition of their effective masses exactly opposite — directly across the grass walk. These phloxes cry aloud for balance, placed as they seem to be in a distinctly formal setting.

So it is in the formal flower garden. I have come to see quite plainly, through several years of lost time, that balanced planting throughout is the only planting for a garden that has any design worth the name. It is difficult to conceive of that formal garden in which the use of formal or clipped trees would be inappropriate; and these we must not fail to mention, not only because of the fine foil in color and rich background of dark tone which they bring into the garden, but because of their shadow masses as well and their value as accents. And that word "accents" brings me to the consideration of the first important placing of flowers in a garden which like my own is, unlike all Gaul, divided into four parts.

Two cross-walks intersect my garden, causing four entrances. To flank each of these entrances, it can be at once seen, balanced planting must prevail. In the eight beds whose corners occur at these entrances, this planting is used: large masses of *Thermopsis Caroliniana* give an early and brightly conspicuous bloom. Around these the tall salmon-pink phlox, Aurore Boreale, much later; below this — filling out the angle of the corner to the very point — the blue lyme grass (*Elymus arenarius*), gladiolus William Falconer, and, lowest of all, *Phlox Drummondii,* var. Chamois Rose. None of these colors fight with each other at any time, and the large group of tall-growing things is well fronted by the intermediate heights of the lyme grass and the gladiolus when in growth or in bloom. The four far corners of my garden I also consider more effective when planted with tall-growing flowers; in these the Dropmore, *Anchusa Italica,* first shines bluely forth; this soon gives place to the white physo-stegia, with phlox Fernando Cortez blooming below the slim white spikes just mentioned; and last, to light up the corners, comes the mauve *Physostegia Virginica,* var. *rosea,* whose bloom here is far more profuse and effective than that of its white sisters. This group-ing gives almost continuous bloom and very telling color from mid-June to mid-September; the periods of green, when they occur, are short, and the vigorous-looking plants are not at all objectionable before they blossom. The effect of balanced planting in these corners I consider good. The eye is carried expectantly from one angle to another and expectation is fulfilled.

In the centre of this garden are four rectangular beds, correspond-ing in proportion to the size of the rectangular pool. These, as forming part of the centre of the garden, are always planted exactly alike. Purple of a rich bluish cast is one of the colors which bind instead of separate, and purple it is which here becomes an excellent focal color for the garden. In the middle of each bed is a sturdy group of the hardy phlox Lord Rayleigh, surrounded on all sides by heliotrope of the darkest purple obtainable. This year, however, I expect to replace the heliotrope with even better effect by a tall blue ageratum, which I saw in one or two Connecticut gardens, as the paler color is more telling and quite as neutral for such a position. Speaking of this ageratum, I may perhaps digress for a moment to mention a charming effect I saw on an out-of-door dining-table last summer, obtained by the use of this flower. The color of the table was a pale cool green and most of its top was exposed; in the centre stood a bowl of French or Italian pottery, bearing a careless gay decoration, and at the four corners smaller bowls. These were filled, to quote the words of the knowing lady whose happy arrangement this was, "with zinnias which had yellows and copper-reds, with the variety which resulted from an order of salmon-pinks and whites. We really had almost everything but salmon-pink."

The zinnias, I who saw them can affirm, made a most brilliant mass of color not altogether harmonious; but all was set right by the introduction, sparingly managed, of the lovely ageratum, Dwarf Imperial Blue. The eye of her who arranged these flowers saw that a balm was needed in Gilead; the ageratum certainly brought the zinnia colors into harmony as nothing else could have done, and a charmingly gay and original decoration was the result. What a suggestion here, too, for the planting of a little garden of annuals!

We are apt to think of balance in the formal garden as obtained for the most part by the use of accents in the shape of formal trees, or by some architectural adjunct. I believe that color masses and plant forms should correspond as absolutely as the more severe features of such a garden. For example, in practically the same spot in all four quarters of my garden there are, for perhaps four to six weeks, similar masses of tall white hardy phloxes, the blooming period beginning with Von Lassberg and closing with Jeanne d'Arc, the white repeated in the dwarf phlox Tapis Blanc in four places nearer the centre of the garden.

For accents in flowers, the mind flies naturally to the use, first, of the taller and more formal types of flowers. Delphiniums with their fine uprightness and glorious blues; hollyhocks where space is abundant and rust doth not corrupt; the magnificent mulleins, notably *Verbascum Olympicum,* might surely emphasize points in design; and I read but now of a new pink one of fine color, which, though mentioned as a novelty in Miss Ellen Willmott's famous garden at Warley, England, will be sure to cross the water soon if invited by our enterprising nurserymen. Lilies of the cup-upholding kinds, standard roses, standard wistarias, standard heliotropes are all to be had. The use of the dwarf or pyramidal fruit-tree in the formal garden is very beautiful to me, recalling some of the earliest of the fine gardens of England, and (where the little tree is kept well trimmed) offering a rarely interesting medium for obtaining balanced effects.

But the tall plants are not the only available means for producing balanced effects. Lower masses of foliage or flowers have their place. They must be masses, however, unmistakable masses. Thus each of the large flower masses of baby's breath (*Gypsophila elegans*) — consisting of the bloom of but a single well-developed plant — is repeated in every instance in four corresponding positions in this garden. In a fine garden in Saginaw, Michigan, designed and planted by Mr. Charles A. Platt, balance is preserved and emphasized in striking fashion by the use of the plantain lily (*Funkia Sieboldii,* or *grandiflora*), with its shining yellow-green leaves. Masses of this formal plant are here used as an effective foreground for a single fine specimen bush, not very tall, of Japan snowball (*Viburnum plicatum*). The poker flower (*Tritoma Pfitzeri*) is also used in this garden to carry the eye from point to corresponding point; and speaking of tritoma, which Mr. Platt in this garden associates with iris, let me mention again that delightful ageratum, as I lately saw it, used below tritoma. The tritoma must have been one of the newer varieties, of an unusual tone of intense salmony-orange, and while the ageratum would seem too insignificant in height to neighbor the tall spike above it, the use of the lavender-blue in large masses added enormously to the effect of the torches.

The rather thin-looking elms seem to flank the garden entrance rather fortunately. A certain pleasurable sensation is felt in the balance afforded by the doubly bordered walk with its blue and lavender Michaelmas daisies or hardy asters. It is surely the repetition of the twos which has something to do with this: two borders, two posts, two trees, the eye carried twice upward by higher and yet higher objects.

MY
GARDEN

---

by
Louise Shelton

1916

L ESS THAN ONE ACRE on a hillside. Two terraces, making two flights of steps between the
house and lower garden. In laying out this small
place, a rather informal planting seemed desirable in
order that the restricted space and boundary lines could

be treated in a manner that might cause them to be unnoticed, more or less. For this purpose a part of the main path was laid out in irregular lines with just enough shrubbery on either side to conceal the curves. This scheme leaves something to the imagination, which interesting sense is sure to exaggerate and to enlarge while the path keeps turning.

In the upper garden, the planting is made rather difficult by the shade of the Apple-trees, although at the risk of the flowers, the gardener has never dreamed of dispensing with anything as cherished as these graceful old trees. On the right, where the shadows are denser, early wild flowers and Narcissi grow, and Forget-me-nots appear with the Apple bloom, followed later by the cheerful Nicotiana affinis and Salvia to enliven the shadows. The little formal planting on the left has the sun after ten in the morning, and many of the perennials and annuals thrive here.

In the lower garden, where there is more sun, there are beds of bloom and groups of tall shrubs. A small, curved path between two Rose beds leaves the main walk to end in a grape arbor, through which a grass path leads to the gardener's bower enclosed by shrubs and "skylighted." This circular green room contains a curved white seat and table, and is a peaceful retreat, inviting book and pen, or other quiet pastime. Elsewhere there are nooks for Lilies-of-the-Valley, bulbs in the grass, and a bird bath, while the eight-room purple martin house stands like a lodge near the gate leading into a lane. Absolute simplicity, cosiness, and privacy prevail, all made possible by a few shrubs, trees, and flowers, and some imagination. Contrasting it now with its original state as a grassy slope bounded with fences, one might say — quoting Mr. Lowell:

> *"Till now one dreamed not what could be done*
> *With a bit of earth and a ray of sun."*

GARDENS THAT ARE AND ARE TO BE

by

Richardson Wright

1922

S OME PAGES BACK I stated that I preferred to garden *coram populo*. I cannot hold with the English theory of enclosing all gardens with walls, because, just as a man may not possess leisure to himself, or live a life to himself, so he cannot make a garden to himself.

Try to keep a garden beautiful to yourself alone and see what happens — the neighbor, hurrying by to catch his train of mornings, will stop to snatch a glint of joy from the iris purpling by your doorstep. The motorist will throw on brakes and back downhill just to see those Oriental poppies massed against the wall.

Nature is always on the side of the public. Build your wall never so high but her winds will carry the seeds of that choice variety you reserved for yourself to a dozen different dooryards and open fields, where they will blossom next season. Plant your hedgerow never so thick but a vine will stretch forth a friendly finger through it. Lock the gate never so tight but the zephyrs will waft odors of rose and hyacinth and mignonette to every passer-by.

It follows, then, that a garden is a public service and having one a public duty. It is a man's contribution to the community. It is not enough that law and order be preserved in our communities. Only the policeman with his truncheon would stand between us and chaos if law and order were all we desired. No, it is the mark of an upward-looking civilization that men make beautiful gardens, that the joy of the tulip and the flowering shrub be shared with other men.

II

This is the philosophy behind the making of the gardens on our seven acres more or less. This was the sort of sentiment we returned to those who suggested our walling in the front lawn with tall shrubs and piling shrubbery along the back of the long herbaceous border. Herbaceous borders should have a background; that is true; but if you cut off your view to the distant hills, if you hide that border's beauty from those coming up your own hill, then you are very much mistaken in your theory of gardening.

This long border was a problem that could have been solved readily had we moved out and the landscapist moved in. But that sort of garden we had no intention of making. So we labored over maps and color schemes and catalogues and battled and argued and questioned and compromised, until, finally, there was evolved a scheme that would give us our favorite flowers in succession of bloom.

We had started by making the backbone of this border a middle row of German iris and peonies, with some of the iris coming well to the front to give the occasional accent of unusual height. English daisies, raised in the upper seed-bed behind the vegetable garden, made an irregular front line, broken here and there with pansies and violas and later-blooming low things, such as sweet alyssum. In one corner, where a fir gave background, was placed a shoal of white phlox, with a mass of delphinium Rev. E. Lascelles beside it. This combination was repeated at the farther end and again in the middle. Foxglove, Canterbury bells, and hollyhocks gave height along the back, with cosmos moved in in late spring from the annual garden. Massed here and there went groups of Japanese iris and some Siberian iris 'Purple King.' Helenium gave us a fall bronze. Bee-balm furnished a deep red in midsummer. Geums in little groups gave brilliant spots of color. I even tempted the ire of garden friends by putting in, in midsummer, little drifts of marigolds, lemon and gold, and white and blue asters to follow along before the Michaelmas daisies. Some few groups of bronze and yellow hardy chrysanthemums further enliven the autumn.

Below the wall, at the top edge of the meadow, and forming a lower tier of this border, is set a long line of tall cosmos and the ubiquitous golden glow, making a tidal wave of color and delicate greenery from July on, punctuated with the significant yellow of the golden glow, the white of early cosmos and, later, the red, pink, and white of the ordinary fall cosmos.

Without a map, which I have no intention of drawing, the scheme of planting cannot be appreciated. It is very unorthodox and disorderly and apparently unkempt. But this is her garden, and she has a penchant for wildish effects. She says that a border shouldn't look as if it had just had a permanent wave.

III

But if there was a jungle effect in color and leafage in the long border, it served a definite purpose — as a contrast to what is beyond. This border runs along a stretch of lawn, and at the end a little planting of cedars develops into a formal garden — her little formal garden. Cedars were taken from Doglands, across the road, and set in their native soil, rank on rank of them, enclose a little spot with grass paths and a burst of color at the end in front of the taller cedars. Here is placed a tiny pool, simple in outline and without pretension, to mirror the stars and clouds and sky, a little jewel — now sapphire, now ruby, now garnet, now topaz — in a setting of green. Every garden should have some form of water, even if it is only a tub sunk in the sod and big enough to hold a water-lily. The garden with running water — a brook, a waterfall — ah, what possibilities! For of the music in the garden none is more lovely than the *pizzicato* of dripping water or the *rondo* of a babbling stream.

The rear cedar wall of this little formal garden is in line with our projected rose garden. Perhaps it is bad taste to repeat one's dreams, to speak of that which the lean purse may never permit one to attain. So far in developing these few acres we have gone on the very bad economic principle of doing what we could not afford and then working day and night to afford it. That is doubtless the way the rose garden will come; I see no other way.

This, if you please, will have a wall, for the simple reason that the slope which is there now faces north, the slope now naturalized to a multitude of narcissus. At the orchard end it will be higher than my head, and in that sheltered position espalier fruit can be trained on the west and north walls. The east wall need not be so high, as it leads off the *tapis vert* behind my study porch. This will be broken by low, broad steps giving gradual approach to the level of the rose garden. On the north side steep stone steps will lead down to the level of the little formal garden; on the south side a gate will open on the kitchen garden. There will be big work in leveling down that slope and a vast expenditure for manure and lime and Scotch soot, but there is no use starting a rose garden unless you start it right. Like a wife, a rose garden is a distinct luxury, and one should not enter upon either of them lightly or without first counting the cost. Not that lovely roses cannot be grown and are grown without a great outlay of money. Better have a few roses in a border than no roses at all.

Or you may look at the rose habit this way — start with a few and learn the simple requirements in handling those few. The beginner stands in terror of the various rose pests and sprays and kinds of mulch and stimulating plant foods that various writers and seedsmen recommend. Like learning German irregular verbs or, what is worse, Russian verbs, every case seems to differ, every little curl of leaf and spot on petal calls for a new kind of spray. It will greatly simplify matters when the beginning gardener finds that most of these sprays can be reduced to one, and that common sense, not deep garden intellectuality, lies behind the various treatments suggested for roses. I feel that this pest and spray side of rose-growing has been exaggerated, and that many people who would otherwise pay a great deal of attention to roses have been scared off.

IV

While the rose garden was held in abeyance, the autumn border went ahead. A broad strip sprawling up the hill alongside the road to the barn and the kitchen garden was turned over for the frosts and snow to sweeten. I watched that plot lovingly through two blizzards and innumerable zero days. For there remained indelibly in my mind a vision I had seen at the Royal Horticultural Society's fall exhibition at Vincent Square the year before — a vision of Michaelmas daisies and hardy chrysanthemums, the like of which I

never knew could be grown. There was also imprinted on that gray matter the picture of many beds of tritoma flaming that fall at Kew. I had made a solemn promise before I left London that somewhere in those seven acres more or less would be built an autumn border where Michaelmas daisies and the hardy pompoms and a range of kniphofia would flourish into Indian summer.

Because they grow wild in our New York and New England meadows we are apt to neglect the possibilities of the starwort asters — the Michaelmas daisies. English nurserymen have developed them with remarkable success, great blossoms, great flurries of clustered blooms that are so beautiful to look upon that you eat your heart out with envy for them. The hardy chrysanthemums, of course, we do grow in abundance, and we need not blush for those shown at our fall flower exhibitions.

The kniphofia, on the other hand, is passing under a cloud just at present. We know them, our landscape architects say, "Oh, yes," when you mention them, and our nurserymen nod knowingly. But they all mention how undecorative the foliage looks, and that seems to be about all there is to it. Trying to be enthusiastic about tritomas just now is like mentioning to a family of the socially elect the wayward small brother who got infatuated with a waitress and married her. They won't say anything against him, but you can gather, from the tone of voice, that they won't say much for him.

The case against tritomas isn't so much the foliage as it is the psychology of their color. We may talk about a heavenly blue delphinium or the fierce red of salvia or the fragile flames of the poppies, and yet it cannot be said that American gardeners are entirely converted to the use of strong color. People still refer to "pastel shades" in the garden. Now, the tritoma is anything but a pastel shade, although many varieties have a subtle blending of red, yellow, and green tones in them. Taken *en masse,* they are bold, strong color. They do not blend gently, they are direct and imposing and vital. Showy? Yes. But we need such showy points for accents in our gardens. We may think them crude and unlovely, but I'm reminded of the fact that the brilliant, contrasting colors one finds in the parks of Paris have a beauty that is remembered when all the pussyfoot pastel blending in other gardens is forgotten. We need some of that direct color in our American gardens, and tritomas will give it.

So this border was made broad and deep, to accommodate perennials that would afford color from midsummer on into the late fall. Poppies are planted at intervals for a succession of bloom — Shirleys and some white annuals saved from a garden in Surrey and some that Luther Burbank has created. Gypsophila florc-pleno marks the transition from color to color. Verbena spreads here and there along the front. Little clumps of annual chrysanthemums add to the midsummer glory. Snapdragons, tawny red and golden brown and yellow, range down the middle of the bed — these also from seeds saved in that Surrey garden. And behind them, astilbe, delphinium, tritomas, statice, Michaelmas daisies, and many dahlias, with lower clumps of the hardy mums in red, claret, white, yellow, and bronze.

Of autumn days I like to climb the hill to my vegetable garden and rest there a moment looking back on this display. It is the last challenge of the year — but what a challenge! What a gorgeous finale, this autumn border!

THE
GARDEN
IN
THE
MAKING

by
Herbert Durand

1927

M Y WILD FLOWER GARDEN occupies
and adorns an area that measures
roughly sixty by one hundred feet. It was
originally just a compact and solid mass of bare, pro-
truding rock. But it was rock that had been carved and
molded by the elements into a remarkable diversity of
contour. There were rounded hills divided by steep-

sided ravines, gentle declivities that sloped from lofty summits to lowland plains, alluring hillocks and bowl-like depressions and, everywhere, crevices and fissures and earth pockets galore. Of course, in such a limited area these topographical features were all on a lilliputian scale, but they fitted perfectly, every one of them, the garden scheme I had in mind.

I had no intention of making a mere rock garden; and it isn't. The idea was to duplicate as best I could on that solid foundation the conditions of soil, moisture and exposure prevailing in the woods and fields and swamps of the surrounding countryside. It looked like an absurd undertaking, but if successful it meant that snug homes could be provided for thousands of native wild flowers and ferns; and that was what I ardently wished to do. Dozens of inquisitive Sunday morning onlookers, when they learned what I was about, told me I never would make it; but I did, and here is the story:

The work was started with an attempt to reproduce a shady woodland slope, and the results were encouraging beyond all expectations. I had neither woodsy soil nor shade, but there were virgin woods all around me that were covered with deep, rich mold and abounded in dogwoods, beeches, oaks and maples, all trees with dense leafage. An old stone wall that a friendly neighbor was about to have hauled away was drawn upon for retaining rocks and to build up pockets. As the stones were exactly like my own outcrop in color and character, and were so placed that their seams and stratifications ran in the same direction as mine, they really looked as if they belonged. And, by avoiding straight rows and breaking the contours with occasional rounded and weather-worn boulders of good size, a notably natural effect was achieved, without the least suggestion of stilted edgings or artificial terraces.

How to prepare and manipulate the soil for the beds that were to cover the naked rock, so it would retain moisture without losing its light, leaf-moldy texture, was a problem that required and was given considerable study. Finally, I discovered that the wild soils of the cliffs, that rested upon a subsoil of clay, were always damp in normal weather, whether they were deep or shallow, while soils without such a foundation quickly dried out. A severe wind storm had uprooted a huge tulip tree just across my line and exposed a mass of yellow clay. This I plastered over the rock bottoms of shallow beds until the layer was two or three inches deep and upon it I dumped black, crumbly mold from the nearby forest to the depths desired.

Finally the rock hollows, admirably located for their purpose, were surrounded with ramparts of heavy stones and depth of from two to three feet of rich loam obtained in each. In them were planted a half dozen fine, bushy dogwoods from eight to ten feet high, several oaks and maples and one thrifty beech. All flourished and the second season my woodland slope was a reality. In its shaded nooks were established colonies of bloodroots, Dutchman's breeches, hepaticas, anemones, trout-lilies, trilliums, Solomon's plume and wood violets. Room was also found for an occasional clump of yellow lady-slippers and showy orchids; and a good number of maidenhair and evergreen wood ferns were added to supply grace and greenery after the spring riots of brighter color are quelled.

At the close of the third growing season the continued prosperity of this bit of planting is very gratifying. The dogwoods have increased in stature and spread, the soil has held moisture like a sponge and the flowers and ferns seem as contented as if they had never been moved.

The high and dry places were next given attention. Most of the rock crevices and pockets were already filled with black mold and in these were tucked away ebony spleenworts, bladder ferns, woodsias, wild pinks, columbines, bluebells, saxifrages and other cliff dwellers, care being taken to give each species its favorite exposure. On the level sunny spots more beds were made and filled with woods earth mixed with a liberal proportion of clean sand; but the yellow clay foundation was omitted. Here were installed native sedums (did you know that there are scores of beautiful kinds?), the wine-

leaf cinquefoil, several mountain pinks, the crowberries, the pink corydalis, and later on, dozens of choice desert and alpine flowers of great charm that were sent me by friends in the South and Far West. Except for two or three somewhat protracted dry spells, there has been sufficient rain every year to supply the needs of all these sun and sand addicts, and the garden hose has rarely been turned in their direction.

At this stage of the work, the necessity of laying out some sort of path system became evident and I decided that stepping stones would be most appropriate and that they should be laid in irregular curves so arranged as to give intimate access to every part of the garden. The remnant of the old wall supplied fine flat stones in sufficient quantity and it did not take many "off" days to place them.

I next proceeded to make a Fernery of the little ravine leading upwards from the door of the sun room to the summit of the big rock. This ravine is in rather deep shade during most of the day. It had been clogged with broken schist and shale during the blasting of the basement. Most of this deposit was dug out and carried away, but enough was left to mix with various soils and give both the ferns and a number of flowering plants just the sort of footing they prefer. Over fifty species of common ferns and a dozen rare kinds and varieties have been happily located there and are now flourishing.

Practically all the work in the new garden that first season was done by myself. My only help was from a lusty Italian, hired occasionally and only to tote heavy rocks and lug in woods dirt. (I soon found that I must supervise his activities in person in order to get the kind of rocks and dirt desired.) Progress was necessarily slow, for Saturdays, Sundays and Holidays were the only days that could be spared from other duties. So it was mid-October before the Fernery was completed, and further constructive effort had to be postponed until the following spring.

The ensuing winter was actually one of the briefest and mildest for many years, but it seemed interminable to me, so impatient was I to resume my fascinating work in the wild garden. I got some satisfaction from building a red cedar fence around the garden on mild days, for it has served to protect my plant treasures from stray dogs and other vandals, particularly Sunday motorists of the breed that considers as its legitimate prey anything found green and grow-ing anywhere outside the city limits. But after Christmas I often found myself counting the days until Saint Patrick's day; and when that blessed occasion at last arrived, nothing, not even predictions that I would "catch my death of cold," could keep me out of the old suit or out of the garden.

I had been learning a lot about soil acidity and had discovered the apparent reason why I had never been able to grow trailing arbutus, pink lady-slippers and other fastidious favorites. So no time was lost in making two beds of intensely acid soil — one in a sunny spot, the other in the shadow of a fine pin oak and two husky hemlocks, the bill for which flattened my pocketbook alarmingly. These beds were filled with earth that had been laboriously scraped from under hemlock trees, earth that was shown by chemical tests to contain over three hundred times as much acid as pure rain water.

And, when summer came, I went on weekly collecting expedi-tions. One was to a northern New Hampshire forest, where speci-mens of the two plants mentioned and of the twin flower, the wood sorrel, the creeping snowberry, the bunchberry and a few other acid-lovers, were located, dug, brought back home, and carefully planted under the hemlocks. These lovely strangers made themselves so

entirely at home in their new quarters that it has been a joy ever
since to see them thriving and even reproducing themselves there
exactly as they would in their natural habitat.

Another undertaking that second year was the making and filling
of three beds, two in full sun, one in shade, for lime-loving species.
The soil was a mixture of well-limed garden loam and an equal
quantity of neutral humus, dug under maples and beeches. Oaks
were avoided as their decomposed foliage is about as acid as that
of hemlocks and pines. These beds were gradually filled with a
goodly assortment of charming rock, desert and prairie plants from
limestone regions.

There yet remained two classes of plants, aquatics and bog dwellers, for which no provision had been made. Strange as it may seem,
my rock contained admirable locations for both a pool and an
artificial bog. Right at the base of the miniature cliff at the southern
edge of the upper plateau was a circular hollow or pot-hole five feet
in diameter, fourteen inches deep and watertight. The depth was
increased to eighteen inches by a rim of oblong stones set in well-
hidden cement along the lower quadrant, and a five-minute flow
from the hose filled the cavity and transformed it into a gem of a
pool all ready for occupancy. It now contains a thrifty pitcher-plant,
a tiny Cape Cod waterlily, a wild calla, a bogbean, a golden marsh
marigold, a snow-white ditto from Colorado that blooms in early
summer, a clump of the narrow-leaved cat-tail, three forms of ar-
rowhead, an enormous bullfrog and four goldfish. As crested and
ostrich ferns, grass of Parnassus, meadow beauties, and bluebells
are thickly planted at the water's edge, bright color is never lacking
here from mid-April until Thanksgiving Day.

Making the pseudo bog was not so easy; in fact even now I have
more swamp plants than swamp; and it is no simple matter to
remember and keep them as well soaked as they should be. The
location is all right but there is something wrong with the make-
up; it doesn't hold water. I was prodding around with a crowbar
one day, hunting deep places for trees, when I struck this hidden

hole in the rock. It proved to be fully four feet deep, with an oval surface area five feet by four; and it was filled with pure leaf mold, the accumulation of many years. It matters not at all what was done or left undone, as it must sometime be done over. Somehow, "sometime" always seems to mean "next spring." The leak must be stopped and yet some way of letting out the water when necessary must be devised. Perhaps a buried length of pipe, emerging farther down the hill and with a spigot at the end, will do the trick. If so the hollow will be emptied, waterproofed by a layer of cement or impervious clay at the bottom, refilled with two feet or so of swamp peat, covered with a mixture of leaf mold and sphagnum moss and saturated with water.

It is going to take several strenuous days to do all this and as it must be done at a time of year when I am always busy with other seemingly more important matters, the job just now resembles more a section of pavement in the fervid place of good intentions than it does impending reality. Meanwhile my almost complete collection of native irises, my bog orchids and other gems from Nature's sanctuaries, that are now ekeing out a precarious existence under adverse conditions, must be cuddled and nurtured and watered watchfully and lovingly and everlastingly. May they live long and prosper, those which survive until "next spring" really comes.

OUR
FIRST
GARDENS

by
Anna Gilman Hill

1938

I NOW REALIZE that these first years were only my novitiate, preparing of myself to build my little gray garden by the sea. For whenever I say *my* garden I mean that small walled garden opening out of the sun-room at Easthampton. In 1913 we bought a gray shingled cottage and four acres of land on Lily Pond Lane in one of the Hamptons. Lily Pond Lane, what a name to conjure with! . . . and there actually were lilies, myriads of them, on the pond. Our acreage was between Georgica Pond and the sea, a part of that low land which was once a bog lying back of the dunes.

This long strip of fertile land runs from Montauk to Shinnecock Bay and on beyond with interruptions towards Jones Beach. It was created especially for gardeners, flower gardeners as well as market gardeners. There is just the proper balance of rich black loam and sand, superb drainage, and almost continuous moisture from the sea to make all green things upon that particular piece of earth praise the Lord with might and main. With their roots reveling and exploring deep down into that mine of stored-up food, a rich black muck of ages past, no wonder their blossoms are larger and more brilliantly colored than those of inland plants.

Gardening in Suffolk County spoils you for gardening anywhere else in North America. It is an almost foolproof place, for all you have to do to grow the most delicate specimen is to go out into the rough lawn or into a field, dig a hole and put it in. In a year, whatever you have planted will be taking a prize at the show. The problem of when to plant, too, is far easier than in a long-season garden. For, as we never were in residence there until June 1st, the first flower needed was the sweet dianthus, fringy white fluffs nestling in their blue-gray leaves. The last flower was the tall *Anemone japonica,* which throve in the shadiest border.

The first year I tried to grow my plants in an open field. They flourished like Jonah's gourd, but the first nor'easter laid them flat. No amount of tying and staking could hold them upright against the scudding sea-spume. A windbreak is the *sine qua non* of seashore gardening. I found, too, that the friable sandy loam was a paradise for brother mole, yea, and for his sisters and his cousins and his aunts. We began to talk of walls with concrete bases which should go below mole-level.

Some paintings by Elizabeth Shippen Green of children playing in an old Pennsylvania walled garden gave me the inspiration for our little garden. I wanted cement walls, high enough in some places to be pierced by arches with clanging wooden doors, the kind of doors that have latches and hinges forged by the local blacksmith. I wanted arches recessed in the wall for seats and a fountain. I visualized a thatched tool house just outside the far gate towards the vegetable garden and I wanted an exedra overlooking the sea. March found us beginning excavations for the foundation walls. A deep narrow trench cut in the level sod and filled with rough cement and cinders formed a rectangle measuring forty by seventy-five feet.

High garden walls are more usual in England than here, and for good reasons. The English vegetable garden is almost always enclosed by high walls, on the southern side of which the fruit ripens in the sun, protected by nets from the depredations of birds. In our Eastern states the dry atmosphere makes the pleaching of fruit trees a dubious practice. Red spider thrives in our long dry spells, and the leaves are apt to curl and fall. But we could use walls to advantage in our seaside gardens. At Luffness in Scotland I once saw a double-walled garden built by the monks in the Abbey garden. It was a large diamond-shaped enclosure surrounding a smaller diamond. The tenderest fruit was grown in the inner close. Fierce gales from the North Sea beat upon those walls, but within all was quiet and very verdant, the trees receiving the benefit of the sea mists and escaping the violent winds.

When walls are impractical for some reason or other, an enclosure of woven wood fence will give an excellent windbreak, and many are the pleasing effects which we can secure with such a background. Large-flowered clematis lend themselves especially well to the covering of these woven fences. Plant them on the west or north side and train them through to the sun. They like to have their lower branches shaded from the too exciting call of the spring sun. They are lime-lovers — never forget their annual dose of powdered limestone mixed with well-decayed manure spring and fall.

It was at Easthampton that I first tried to grow the large-flowered clematis which embower the gardens of England. At first I had no success. Then I realized that our seashore soil was too acid. Liberal additions of powdered limestone and old waste rubble thoroughly incorporated in the soil rectified the condition, and we had no trouble in clothing the walls with magnificent specimens of white Henryi and Nelly Moser.

We were our own architects, but the village carpenter made the

wooden forms which were set upon the foundation walls, and the local mason literally poured and molded our little Gray Garden into shape. It was a good job. No rodent ever undermined those walls; no nor'easter ever toppled over a plant within them nor tore away the vines. Flexible lead holders for these had been driven into the walls while the cement was soft. To attach the vines still more firmly and at the same time afford shade for the arched seats, we contrived iron brackets to clasp down for twelve inches over the coping, carrying an adjustable thirty-inch arm on one side. On this, one could loop up roses or clematis and throw the shadow wherever it was desired.

The pillars of the little exedra were molded in cement in tin. That was a mistake. A metal container gives too smooth a finish to the cement. When we made the cement pillars for the pergola at Niederhurst a few years later we had the carpenter construct the mold of perpendicular scantlings which gave a pleasing and classic fluted effect on the shaft of the column.

The garden was about two or three hundred yards from the sea; between lay a rough pasture of bayberry and wild roses. A low gate in the rear of the exedra opened onto a path to the beach through the dip of the dunes. I close my eyes and sense again the scent of those wild roses, the caress of the hot sun on our backs as we sauntered to and fro from our bath and lazy mornings on the beach. Many were the lawnmowers put out of commission by my husband in the making of that path! When we left it ten years later it was a velvet carpet from garden to dune.

Sitting in the garden, you had a glimpse of blue water between the dunes; high dunes, grass-covered and soft gray like our walls.

I could find no wall fountain to suit me so I secured a graceful circular bird bath on a pedestal. This particular one was called a "second" at the terra cotta works. A flaw on one side of the bowl reduced its cash value but not its beauty when I set the wounded side deeply into the cement of the concrete wall and produced just the effect I was after. It was such a success that a few years later the manufacturers made the same model for me but with the side of the basin nicely flattened, so I could use it against the stone wall at Niederhurst.

The blue-green gates clanged merrily in their wide low arches. There were two on the side toward the house, both flanked by gray jars of blue hydrangeas. Hydrangeas naturally turn a luminous pale blue at the Hamptons owing to the large amount of iron in the water. In Suffolk County if you want to keep your pink ones their original color you must never give them anything but rain water to drink.

A few years later we added a garden room or sun-room on the south side of the house and joined it directly to the garden by a wide planted pathway flanked with parallel walls three feet high. By doing this we could literally live in the garden. It became a part of the house. Never before or since have I been so intimate with my flowers as here in this blessed sun-room.

It was a very sunny garden. Few trees will grow in that wind-swept section and as I had had enough of tree roots and shade at home, the flowers and I reveled in the open situation. It was small, convenient and near at hand, and, best of all, I could easily take care of it myself. Although I had no regular gardener, Edward Tidridge, who has lived with us for over twenty years as guide, philosopher, chauffeur and maître d'hôtel, and is himself a keen gardener, attended to the tasks (in his odd hours) which were too difficult for me, such as the spring digging and untangling of luxuriant rose vines.

In May, we used to take a hurried trip down from the city, planted the hardy annual seeds thinly, sheltered them on the east by low boards, and left them, with a prayer, to care for themselves until June. We repaired the winter damage and dug well-decomposed manure around all perennials and vines.

It was truly a gray garden. The soft gray of the dunes, cement walls and sea mists gave us our color scheme as well as our name. We used as edgings all the low gray-foliaged plants such as nepeta, stachys, and pinks. Clipped bushes of santolina, lavender and rosemary made gray mounds here and there. Only flowers in pale colors were allowed inside the walls, yet the effect was far from insipid.

The valuable pale yellow tone of *Thalictrum glaucum* and *Digitalis ambigua* blended exquisitely with pale pink *Phlox drummondi* and scabiosa. Later, shell-pink phlox Mme. Paul Dutrie bloomed with aster Queen Mary, a particularly happy juxtaposition, as was the later white digitalis with *Delphinium belladonna*.

Lupines, which had refused to do anything for me elsewhere, thrived in this gentle sandy loam. Great creamy masses of these temperamental blossoms, both annual and perennial, made foreground for tall early asters. Here I worked with hybrid delphinium, which luxuriates in the deep sand and muck soil and cool nights; trying all the English seed available at the time and later the Hood River strain. I have never been able to get such tall sturdy plants or glorious color in delphinium as we had in this little walled garden so close to the sea.

And, all around, the gray walls were lightly hung with pink, white, and yellowish roses — Trier with its miraculously beautiful stems of foliage, Dr. Van Fleet, Miss Helyatt, and Gardenia. They throve so valiantly that they had to be replanted the third year on the outside of the wall, where they could climb up and form an encircling corona peeping over into the peaceful little close.

Madonna lilies, than which there is nothing more ethereal among created things, gave us their full beauty in July. Here, for once, they were safe from moles and mice.

The true garden is a haven for quiet work and friendly communion, "the world's sweet inn from strife and wearisome turmoil." The very word "garden" denotes an enclosure, and in this walled and friendly little place I realized my ideal.

It would have been harder to leave this garden had it not been that an unforeseen quirk of fortune led us back to the old home on the Hudson. The reason for our coming to this land of beauty had been the illness of a dear member of the family — when that reason no longer held us, we decided to sell both Beechgate and Gray Gardens, buy a permanent shelf in the city in which to hibernate during the winters, and move as much of the garden as we could back to Niederhurst.

Blessed be perennial plants, shrubs, and rose-bushes, the seasoned travelers of plant life. Tall white lilacs which originally came from a friend's old place at Ossining were uprooted and are now blooming profusely under my father's window at Fern Lodge. One of each of my choicest plants traveled back with us. A pale coral Oriental poppy, of which I brought home only one root, has been divided and divided and her progeny now fill the back of the iris terraces just as the bronze iris, Ambassador, is in full bloom. The clematis vines have missed the sandy soil and moisture, but with limestone and sand I have been able to make them less unhappy. The lupines pined away. Many of the plants were as homesick as I for the fresh sea air, and have adapted themselves very slowly to the clay of our northern slope. But many of the roses and crab-apples, lilacs, peonies, and iris are now growing happily in the old garden at Neiderhurst with their grandchildren around their knees.

SEPTEMBER 24, 1960

---

by
Katharine S. White

1960

B Y AUGUST A FLOWER GARDEN, at least on the coast of eastern Maine, where I live, can be at its best — and at its worst. Most of one's successes are apparent, and all of one's failures. For me, this year, heavy memories remain from spring of the disaster area in the north bed of old-fashioned roses, where field mice, hungry under a snowdrift, stripped the bark off the bushes and killed two-thirds of them. Like all disaster areas, this one is still, although replanted, rather bleak. A more recent sorrow is the sudden death on the terrace of a well-established Jack-

mani clematis, which turned black overnight just as its big purple blossoms were opening. There are numerous theories in the household about this loss — too heavy a dose of fertilizer, too much watering, too strong a spray drifting over from the nearby rose beds, a disease still undiagnosed. My own theory is dachshund trouble. Our dachshund is a robin-and-bee hound, not a badger hound. A robust dog, he flings himself with abandon at birds, bees, and fireflies. Once he caught a barn swallow on the wing. Bees swarm all over the clematis bed, attracted by the petunias and violas, the foxgloves and lilies that we grow in front of the clematis, to give the vines the recommended "cool root run." I think the dachshund mortally wounded the Jackmani vine in a scuffle with a bee, for the other large-flowered clematis vines in that bed are spreading their mauve and mulberry stars all over the cedar windbreak, and the roses are in their second surge of bloom. The terrace, despite its accident, is one of our successes, and so, it would seem, are the long borders of perennials, with their masses of hardy phlox, which, because it is mid-August, are in full color. Yet a closer look at the borders will show that even here all is not well. The wars of aggression that I thought our private Security Council and its little army of two, armed with spade, fork, and trowel, had settled in early spring have started again. The lolloping day lilies have begun to blot out the delicate columbines, the clumps of feathery white achilleas are strangling the far more precious delphiniums, and the phlox itself is at the throats of the lupines and the Canterbury bells. Even the low plants at the front of the borders are making aggressive sorties. The ajuga, whose small blue spires were so beautiful in June and early July, is one of the worst offenders. Unless I soon repress its insinuating roots, there will be no violets, pansies, or pinks next year. (I should have known better than to plant the stuff in the first place; after all, the ajuga's familiar name, bugleweed, carries its own warning.) There is also internecine warfare among the phlox — between the burgeoning clumps of common pink, white, and calico phlox and the less well-established stands of the newer varieties, whose colors are more interesting. Nonetheless, I am happy with all this bountiful bloom, and, careless gardener that I am, I comfort myself with the thought that at least I have achieved a mass effect, and that the flowers grow in drifts of color in a way

that even Gertrude Jekyll, the author of *Colour in the Flower Garden*, might have approved. But that formidable garden genius of the last generation would never, never have condoned my crowded beds or my state of August sloth, which makes me want to say, "Oh, let it go. Let the plants fight their own battles."

It is in moods like this that a garden of flowering shrubs seems wonderfully easy and peaceful. Shrubs grow slowly. They need less care, less adjudication, less ruthless cutting back than perennials. We have never grown many shrubs here, probably because a well-landscaped shrubbery does not seem to suit our rural countryside. We do have a few, but they are the common ones, seen on almost every farm — lilacs, spiraea, honeysuckle bush, and shrub roses. Yet flowering shrubs are dear to me. I grew up in a house where the beauty of the shrubbery far surpassed that of the flower beds. We actually lived on a Hawthorn Road, in a suburb of Boston, and the street was named for the three huge English hawthorn trees that grew in our own yard — a red, a pink, and a white. Towering above the lilacs in the curving bed of shrubs, they were a sight to see in May. Only the most ambitious nursery catalogues seem to list hawthorn any more, and when they do they are apt to spell it "hawthorne," such is the carrying power of Nathaniel. To reach our May blossoms, we children had to carry a stepladder into the empty lot next door, use it for the first boost up, and then scramble the rest of the way to a narrow ledge on top of an enormously high lattice fence that backed our shrubbery. Standing there perilously, trying to keep our balance, we had to reach *up* to break the branches. Memory makes the fence at least twenty feet high, and the hawthorn trees many feet higher, but remembered Boston snowdrifts still tower way over my head, so perhaps our hawthorns were only the average height of eighteen or twenty feet. At that, they were the tallest of the shrubs.

Most people do not pick their flowering shrubs, but we always did. I can remember the succession of flowering branches, plucked by the adults of the household and arranged by them in a tall gray Chinese jar, in our gold-and-green parlor. My sister and I and our friends had a game we played with the shrubbery. It was called Millinery. All the little girls in the neighborhood would bring to our lawn their broad-brimmed straw school hats, which, because they were Boston girls' hats, had only plain ribbon bands for decoration. Then each of us would trim her straw with blossoms from the shrubs. There was a wide choice of trimmings — forsythia, Japanese crab, Japanese quince, mock orange, flowering almond, lilac, hawthorn, bridal wreath, weigela, deutzia, with its tiny white bells, and, in June, altheas and shrub roses. We were not allowed to pick the rhododendrons or the azaleas, but nothing else was forbidden. When our flowery concoctions were completed, we put them on our heads and proudly paraded into the house to show them off to our elders; it seems to me now that we must have made quite a gay sight. By dusk the trimmings were dead, and the next day we could start all over again.

THE
SECOND
GARDEN

by
Thalassa Cruso

1971

ONE OF THE MAJOR CHANGES of direction in my gardening life was brought about by the acquisition of a second garden. For a considerable number of years we had a great deal of enjoyment from year-round occupation of the suburban garden. Slowly, by trial and error, it had turned into an all-purpose, well-kept, and reasonably well-organized yard, with room for many different activities. Then, unexpectedly, a change occurred in our way of life, and we decided to look for a house by the water where we could spend the summers. In theory we knew exactly what we wanted: a sound roof over our heads in a small community where the children could roam safely. I also wanted the surrounding property to be in a natural unimproved condition so there would be no garden care. At the back of my mind I had vague plans for an eventual modern garden of my own design, but this was all to be in the very distant future when the family took less time. For the moment, if I had to leave the suburban garden, over which I had worked hard, for the entire summer, I wanted to be free of additional hot-weather gardening.

With this in view, we set out on a house-hunt that took several years, and anyone who has gone through the process knows what follows. Everything we saw was too expensive, in the wrong place, or totally unsuitable. While we searched we rented summer houses, which stiffened my resolve to have nothing to do with summer gardening on a part-time basis. Then one cold, bright day in April we were taken to see a house available for rental in a small seaside community. This house was the complete antithesis of all our requirements. It was a perfectly enormous peeling old ark, surrounded by a tangled, impenetrable wilderness that could easily have contained the bower of Sleeping Beauty without anyone noticing. There was a big, neglected lawn in which ankle-high dead grass rustled in the cold wind off the sea, and an overwhelming air of neglect hung over the place like a shroud. The agent told us that the house had been built and occupied during the summer months by the same family for over fifty years, and that, after the widow of the original owner became elderly and less active, the place had been devastated by two hurricanes. Some attempt apparently had been made to tidy up after the first disaster, but almost nothing had been done after the second, more destructive hurricane, which had taken place three years previously. Since the death of the owner, the house had been rented to summer tenants.

We looked it over with the utmost gloom. For though we were

anxious to find some place for the coming summer, we had grave doubts about spending even a single temporary season in such a house. The rooms were dark; the furniture was creaking wicker; and the beds were iron, with mattresses that defied the possibility of sleep. Some of the floors tilted menacingly where the foundations had been undermined by the sea, and the front porch was so splintered and broken that a chart was needed to make safe passage across it.

But if the house was in bad shape, it shone by comparison with the garden. This covered a huge acreage, most of which was still a litter of broken tree branches at the foot of dead trees all entangled in a confusion of brambles. The front of the yard seemed originally to have been surrounded by a large shrub hedge, but, even in the leafless state of early spring, it was obvious that this was completely smothered by a strangling growth of Japanese honeysuckle and bittersweet. Bittersweet had also been allowed to scramble up one side of the house, where it had reached a jack-in-the-beanstalk height of twisted stems climbing up over each other to form a haven for abandoned birds' nests, the paper lanterns of hornets' nests, and heaven knows what else.

On the other side of the house, a rank, unpruned wisteria had pulled away most of the old-fashioned wooden gutters. This had also penetrated inside a screen porch and was adventuring under the shingles into the house itself. To one side, there was a large unpruned privet hedge enclosing what appeared to be the remains of a rose garden. The rose bushes stood tall, stark, and half dead in the cold April light. And it was all too obvious that the soil in which they were planted had been totally neglected. Behind the overgrown lawn, there were remains of a large vegetable garden enclosed by what once had been a cordon of espaliered apple trees. These were a mass of unpruned growth with only a rusty wire framework to show where once the branches had been trained. On the far side of the big lawn there was a small, freestanding wilderness into which I was advised not to go because it was full of poison ivy. In it, the agent assured me, there was a pond. Leading up to the front door from the road was a straight walk with two large flowerbeds on each side — both knee-high with the uncut stalks of years of inattention. The whole desolate scene was topped off with a derelict little greenhouse full of broken panes of glass.

Nothing less promising could be imagined, except for one thing. Along the side of the property line there was a ditch almost completely obliterated with litter and overgrown, unpruned bushes. Pushing their way through the encompassing jungle were hundreds of daffodils; I could just see them as a yellow streak, but, even under such unpromising conditions, the clumps looked bigger and healthier than any naturalized daffodils I had seen since I left England. The lack of any alternative choice and those daffodils — for the agent cagily plunged into the thicket and picked me an armful — combined to force our hand. Reluctantly we signed a summer lease, stipulating firmly that we would do nothing about the garden except mow the lawn.

During the early part of the summer, I spent most of the time at the beach and paid very little attention to my surroundings. But old habits die hard, and, since I had to pass that area daily, I did cut the privet hedge and prune the roses. Their miserable appearance got on my nerves. The hot weather brought on a fearful infestation of Japanese beetles to add to the garden woes, and I remember my mother, who was staying with us, remarking that she did not envy whoever eventually took on the job of trying to pull this wilderness into shape.

But as the summer wore on, something about that battered old garden began to speak to us. Even in decay it had great dignity, and the more I poked around, for by now my curiosity was getting the better of my intentions, the more evidence I found of an earlier careful plan. There were, for example, a few unusual trees that had survived the hurricanes, including the superb copper beech. I found some good varieties of climbing roses fighting for their lives on a trellis among the invading bittersweet. And late in the summer, in spite of the beetles, the pruned rose garden rewarded me with a few flowers. When I gingerly poked my way in among the poison ivy, I discovered the carved stone head of a lion which once had served as a fountain. In yet another tangle of honeysuckle there was a sundial.

Though I was interested, I was far from ready to become involved. And even though we had by now discovered that the place was for sale, I did not want to take on a ruined house as well as a desolate garden. Our sights were still set on a small place with a naturalistic area around it. Then one wet day, poking around among the rented furniture, I came across an old blanket box in which books had been stored to get them out of the way of summer tenants. One of these looked familiar and turned out to be an English horticultural treatise which had been the mainstay of one of my gardening aunts. The rest were also gardening books, and the collection added up to a considerable number of old-fashioned but well-considered gardening manuals all marked with the date when they had been bought. Leafing through them, I noticed that there were plans and penciled notes in many of the margins. Since rented houses are not noted for the interest of the books they contain, I took them all downstairs to read.

After I had got the years when the books had been purchased into chronological order, I discovered that I had stumbled onto a sort of horticultural treasure trove, for they told the story of the stages in which the ruined garden had been constructed. The house itself had been built in 1898, very much the same time as our suburban house, and the owners had immediately set to work laying out a garden, buying these books to help them with their ideas. The various pencil sketches that appeared in some of the margins showed how the ideas evolved. The first plans were rather simple — the work of youngish people. The increasing sophistication of the garden design showed up clearly as they became more experienced — and also as they bought more complicated gardening books! It made fascinating reading, and it also cleared up a lot of questions that I had not been able to solve from my own investigation of the overgrown areas. Apart from the plans, which were rough and faint, the penciled notes included lists of plants that had been tried, and some rather brisk comments on them: "Nonsense, grows well here" beside a warning that a special plant was hard to handle; "Hideous color, do not recommend" against another overenthusiastic description. The record of over forty years of gardening in one place was there for the searching, and the sense of rediscovery made it all great fun. There was one note to which I felt I must add a postscript. The original entry read "Spring 1905, planted wisteria against the house, hope it grows." I felt compelled to add, "Spring 1946, it did."

This cache of books increased the influence that the old garden was slowly exerting on me. Another wet day I went down to the far end of the lot to investigate an old shed that I was told had been the tool shed in the days of plentiful garden help. Now that the tenants were the gardeners, it was no longer used, and the hand mower we unwillingly pushed across all that grass was kept much closer to hand. In that rather desolate building I found a great variety of excellent gardening tools and equipment, far better than any I had seen since I started gardening in the United States. Much of it was rusty but it had obviously seen hard use.

The personality of the writer of those penciled notes now became much clearer. These were not the tools of a casual gardener but the equipment of an accomplished horticulturalist; indeed, I later discovered that the old garden had been a well-known showplace in its prime. Standing there among the dust and cobwebs, I could imagine all too vividly how the creator of the garden must have felt in her later inactive years, watching her well-ordered garden going to ruin because there was no manpower available, owing to the war, to clear away the wreckage of hurricanes or to do the work she could no longer undertake.

By now I was getting more emotionally involved with this aged white elephant than seemed sensible, and since the summer was coming to an end, it seemed better to put it out of our minds. At the end of the tenancy, I put the gardening books back in the blanket box, picked myself some roses, to which I felt entitled, for there would have been none without that pruning, and firmly shut the door forever on that desolation.

Back in town we set off on another round of house-hunting, but something had gone out of the search and we both knew it. No matter what we saw, we now found we were comparing it with that preposterous derelict old house and garden. Eventually we decided to look it over a final time, telling ourselves that seeing it cold and empty, with the lawn again unmown, would get it finally out of our systems. We went down on Columbus Day, which was fine and hot, and had a picnic lunch on the swaying porch. The bittersweet rampaging everywhere was a mass of red and orange berries; flaming vermilion strands of Virginia creeper were tangled among the dead trees; the sea showed Mediterranean blue across the unmown lawn, and the house was as impossible as ever.

As we sat there debating what to do, the old garden played its trump card. Unexpectedly, we suddenly noticed big clumps of autumn crocus thrusting up among the verges of the overgrown hedges and shining out in the neglected flowerbeds. These indomitable little bulbs have always meant a great deal to me, for in them, more than any other plant, I see the forgiving promise of spring. It was impossible not to be moved to see them still there, in spite of all that had happened to the rest of that yard, carrying on the tradition of the garden that once had been.

We bought the house, and it has been a headache and a haven ever since. We were not able to afford all the land, and I still regret the espaliered trees which went with the piece we did not take. The details of how the garden was restored, and has subsequently been changed, have been described elsewhere. Here it is enough to say that the work, which continues to this day, would never have been possible if I had not first had the chance to learn the basics of gardening in this climate in the suburban yard. Without that experience, the job confronting us in the country garden might have seemed so overwhelming that we would not have bought the house in spite of the autumn crocus.

But it took a lot of effort, for with a growing family there were strict limits on the amount of time available for gardening. Our work in this garden was also confined to the summer months, for at first there was no heat in the house. So for years I felt as though the jungle was only just being held at bay. Then about the period that I was at last getting the upper hand, we took on another immense problem. While I struggled to bring back the country garden, I occasionally rested from my labors and walked across a little bridge that connected our yard to the one next door, in order to enjoy an immaculate garden. This was a house identical in vintage to our own, with a huge piece of lawn and many flowerbeds all beautifully kept up by a resident gardener. After many years of invalidism the owner died, and the very extensive land and woods belonging to the house then fell vacant. I watched with dismay the speed with which a beautiful garden and lawn collapsed during the long drawn-out job of settling a complicated estate. Eventually the heir to the property put the land up for sale for subdivision, and for self-protection we bought the large portion that adjoined our land. In so doing, we reopened a Pandora's box of garden problems that I hoped had been settled forever, for once again I had a decayed garden on my hands crying out for help.

By this time, I had regular garden help, and together we converted this extra piece of land into an integral part of the country place. The house there eventually had to be pulled down; we could find no one to take it away, and we had no use for it. Slowly the land that had belonged to it was transformed to fit into our style of gardening rather than the immaculate but very old-fashioned way in which plants had been grown there previously.

This piece of land brought us plenty of new problems, including one of the few still healthy elms in the entire village, with which we have struggled ever since. It also doubled the amount of land to be cared for. But in compensation it brought us new delight, a small piece of woodland that proved to be a flyway for migrating birds. This third garden was also the source of many new gardening ideas and produced some fundamental changes in my approach to gardening. Rather curiously it still retains a rather different personality. It was never the garden of a horticulturalist, as ours had been; rather, it had been a "well-kept-up place," which is something very different. But it has added enormously to our pleasure, and a garage on the property has provided us with a guest house where we now can spend weekends all year round.

By now I am finished with taking neglected gardens under my wing. There was a frightening period when we found ourselves the owners of yet a fourth enormous piece of land. But by then we had at last learned to say "no more," and we sold this off, though I must, in truth, report that we did keep a small stretch of its waterfront. We are still wrestling with it, and there is a long way to go before that is finally cleaned out! I would not willingly give up an inch of our gardens and there is not an inch that I don't know as well as my own hand. This is how it should be with gardens and gardeners. They should love what they own, and own what they love; but their gardens must never own them, for there will be no pleasure in them if they do.

BLUES

by
Eleanor Perényi

1 9 8 1

I MUST DECLARE AN INTEREST. Whatever the reasons (and I don't think anyone knows or has studied why people respond to colors as they do — snobbery aside, there are unplumbed depths in the psyche that affect whole nations: why do the liberty-loving choose blue and white for their flags, while those who opt for tyrants invariably prefer red and black?) I love blue more than any other color. I am inordinately attracted to any blue substance: to minerals like turquoise and lapis lazuli, to sapphires and aquamarines; to cobalt skies and blue-black seas; to Moslem tiles — and to a blue flower whether or not it has any other merit.

Take anchusa, the Italian bugloss, a hairy perennial that looks like an outsize borage (which it is) and does little credit to the well-groomed border. But an anchusa in bloom is like a Christmas tree with lights so intensely azure they shine out clear across a garden, and I always keep at least one. I harbor the royal blue perennial cornflowers (*Centaurea montana*) for the same reason and in spite of their floppy, undistinguished foliage; and over some opposition (my mother can't abide their prickly, bristly appearance), the steel-blue globe thistle (*Echinops*), whose unopened buds are little balls covered with spikes, miniatures of those weapons one sees in the medieval armory. I doubt if I would care for the veronicas, which are somewhat nondescript and require to be massed to make an effect, if they didn't come in a variety of stained-glass window blues (the pinks and whites leave me cold); and I wouldn't tolerate the invasive, floppy *Tradescantia virginiana* (spiderwort) if it weren't for the cultivar Blue Stone. (Save the tradescantias for rough spots where you want a little color — they don't belong in a border.)

All the above have the advantage of being tough as well as blue. They are perennials you can plant and more or less forget. What they lack is the elegance that doesn't necessarily go with hardiness. For that combination among the blues I look first to the campanulas, especially *C. persicifolia*, the peach-leaved bellflower that will produce flush after flush of enchanting bloom on the wiry stems if you have the patience to go out every morning and remove the faded flowers. These campanulas need only to have their basal rosettes divided every so often to last practically forever, and they are my favorites, though fancier, doubled varieties exist. (*C. glomerata*, dark purple, is one, and to my mind the flowers are too heavy for the stalks.) The same plant in little is *C. carpatica*, and I like it too. Both are to be had in white as well.

Platycodons (blue, white, and a dim pink) are next. Closed, they are lanterns, and they open into stars. Platycodons, too, will be with you forever if you remember where they are and don't wield a careless trowel in early spring. They vanish over winter and don't emerge until mid-May, camouflaged as baby asparagus, and if these easily overlooked shoots are damaged they are done for. Otherwise, they come up in the same place year after year, don't encroach on their neighbors, must not be divided. (Many gardeners get the idea that all perennials should be split up after a few years, often with fatal results. If the clump doesn't increase in size, leave it alone. I lost the best flaxes I ever had, and the only ones to last longer than two years, because some demon whispered that the time had come to separate them; and since that day I have learned to look twice at the structure and growth habits of plants before I start moving them around. In general, those that want dividing will have already started the process for themselves, forming obviously distinct offsets. Those that don't do this, or go to ground leaving no trace, should be left to their own devices — unless, of course, they are bulbs or rhizomes, like iris, which must always be divided.)

Other blue perennials, as handsome as they are durable, that shouldn't be tampered with once established, are the monkshoods and *Baptisia australis*, the false indigo. Monkshoods (*Aconitum*) are tall, elegant plants with glossy, deeply incised foliage and hel-meted flowers. Most bloom in the fall, like shade and have a slightly sinister air, perhaps because one knows they are poisonous. "Very dangerous if eaten or if their juices get into scratches," one authority advises. To my knowledge, neither animal nor child has ever nibbled on my thirty-five-year-old clumps, and my hands, perpetually scratched like those of most gardeners, have survived unscathed the staking, tying, cutting down of the stalks. But it is a thing to know, and I pass it on. The baptisia poses no such problem. It can be a great big perennial, the size of a small shrub, and it is covered with pea-like flowers that are the true indigo blue. (Though called false, the baptisia must be related to the true indigo, which it resembles, because the stems will, I read, produce a weak blue dye.) These and one or two other stand-bys — Virginia bluebells, the powder-blue *Phlox divaricata*, both semi-wildings; Stokes's asters, fringed like sea-anemones — complete the list of blue perennials in residence here. Now for the trouble-makers, those I can't grow for the life of me.

The giant delphiniums come first. I don't mean the garland larkspurs (Belladonna and Bellamosum, light and dark blue respectively, are the classics), nor the Chinese species, nor Connecticut Yankee, developed by the photographer Edward Steichen. All these are of moderate height with loosely organized flowers like big larkspurs, very pretty and easy to grow — if I couldn't succeed with a flower called Connecticut Yankee, I really would die of shame — and given my contempt for the grosser hybrids, they should do me nicely. Alas, where delphiniums are concerned, good taste flies out the window. I want the biggest and showiest, those rulers of the race whose densely packed spires can reach to six feet, the glory of the English herbaceous border. I can do without the pinks and purples. The myriad blues are what I want, all the sapphires and azures of a Chartres window, and an occasional white.

It is hopeless. Delphiniums like a cool damp climate, neither too hot nor too cold, and a sweet soil, what the English call a chalk garden. (Does anyone remember the play of that name and the entrance of Gladys Cooper in a floppy hat, limp dress, garden basket of the type called a Sussex trug over her arm — or have I invented the trug? — deathlessly beautiful at age seventy? Eighty? When I think of delphiniums, that apparition comes back to me.) I supply the lime they need, surround their tender shoots with ashes to keep off slugs, water them tenderly. I tie the stalks individually to slim bamboo poles. The commoner types respond handsomely, but not the giants. They bloom once and never again. I tell myself the climate is at fault, and to an extent that is true. The giant delphiniums thrive along the Maine coast and in the Pacific northwest, home of the Pacific hybrids that even the English now carry in their catalogues, for they are the world's best. Here, better gardeners than I am treat them as biennials and start them early under glass.

I can't do that and excused myself accordingly — until a few years ago when I pulled up to a derelict gas pump on a nearby back road, magnetized by the sight of five-foot delphiniums (and columbines nearly as large) growing in a grassy little pasture that showed no sign of having been cultivated. Queried, the rustic who ran the pump allowed that he raised them both from seed he got from an English firm called Thompson & Morgan. Had I heard of it? I had. At that time it had no American outlet, and I was rather smug about having got hold of a catalogue. Their delphinium seed (Blackmore & Langdon hybrids, the equivalent of our Pacific giants) hadn't done badly either. It was and is the most viable I have tried and once produced a respectable stand that lasted all of three years, a record, but nothing like these beauties in bloom among the weeds. How *he* had got hold of a catalogue was impossible to ask without implying an insulting incredulity. All I could do was humbly ask to buy a few plants, which naturally died on me, and to speculate that the real right way to cultivate giant delphiniums is to scatter the seed in an unplowed field.

Then there is the dustily blue *Catananche caerulea*: Cupid's dart, a daisy with a purple splotch and petals trimmed with pinking shears. Catananches aren't much to look at individually. They should be grown in large clumps drifting through a border, as I first saw them in an Oxford college garden — a garden that also had two white peacocks trailing their fans across a faultless lawn. The lawn and the peacocks are beyond me to imitate. The catananches ought not to be. They aren't rare plants, yet I can't grow them in sufficient quantity to make those blue clouds, or make them last. They tolerate the seed bed; they won't endure transplanting to the perennial beds, and that is that.

Still, they can't be classified as total disasters. I reserve that category for, first, *Meconopsis betonicifolia*, the fabled Himalayan poppy, the color a summer sky, with golden anthers — and my abominable snowman. It grows in England but I have never seen it — not the tiniest shoot having come up from repeated sowings. (Nurseries don't carry it: poppies of this type are notoriously difficult to transplant.) I would give anything for a glimpse of it, even in somebody else's garden. The fact that nobody I know or have heard of grows it ought to console me. *Wyman* says this poppy "always makes a great impression on American tourists visiting England, for it is practically unknown in the U.S.," and I would bet that it is practically unknown in the Himalayas, too, these days, given the record of third-world countries in stripping their forests and wilderness lands, a record considerably worse than our own. What I can't understand is why, if it is practically unknown in the U.S., the seeds are sold by a number of companies. Somebody, somewhere, is cultivating this elusive blue papaver. It is clear I never will.

Another total failure is the gentians. One thinks of these as wild flowers, but some are in cultivation and can be found at nurseries, and since the wild gentians are all on the endangered-species list, growing them in the garden may be the only way to preserve them. I can't do it. There was a moment when I had four little *G. septem-fidae* in the seed bed, a whole year old. These aren't the most exciting of the gentians, not to be compared with the exquisite fringed gentian (*G. crinita*) that is now almost extinct. But I am not fussy and was looking forward to transplanting my little specimens to a spot under the apple tree. Some unknown force put an end to that hope, and I didn't see them again.

Meanwhile I have embarked on yet another, probably doomed

project. It is now my ambition to grow agapanthus, the so-called lily-of-the-nile, not a lily and with no connection to the Nile. (It comes from South Africa.) The flowers are blue or white, and it used to be considered a pot plant only, the tubers to be stored indoors over winter. Now, however, a hardy strain has been developed (*A. orientalis*) which we are promised will grow outdoors, with some protection, where temperatures don't fall below zero. Absent for some years from Wayside's catalogue, these were offered again in 1980 and I ordered the blue, which now sit in the perennial bed. They didn't bloom the first summer and don't have the air of looking forward to their winter season. Neither do I. Something tells me they won't make it. In that case I will try something else. There is no shortage of frustrating blue perennials. I might have another go at the maddening little shrub called caryopteris, a kind of spirea that bursts into a cobalt-blue bloom at summer's end, a time when other blue flowers are absent or hard to come by. *C. x clandonensis*, Heavenly Blue, is the variety to order, and reorder. Three have been given homes here and quickly made their exit to a better world. According to *Wyman*, in a curiously worded sentence, caryopteris "may be killed back by severe winters and, if not, a severe pruning in early spring will usually force it to produce better flowers." Which seems to mean that being killed back is good for them. Mine haven't taken this view, and as for pruning them, they haven't given me the opportunity. Once killed back, they have chosen to leave it at that.

BIOGRAPHIES

Thalassa Cruso (b. 1909) spent most of her childhood in Surrey, England, and came to the United States in 1935. She was well known for her television series "Making Things Grow," which premiered in fall 1967. The garden she describes as her "second" was in Marion, Massachusetts. Her books include *Making Things Grow: A Practical Guide for the Indoor Gardener* (1969), *Making Things Grow Outdoors* (1971), and *To Everything There Is a Season* (1973).

Herbert Durand (1859–1944) lived in Bronxville, New York. In his early career he was a reporter for the *Louisville Courier-Journal*. He lectured and wrote about flowers and was a frequent contributor to magazines. An authority on native wild plants, he wrote several books, including *Taming the Wildings* (1923), *Wild Flowers and Ferns* (1925), *My Wild Flower Garden* (1927), and *Field Book of Common Ferns* (1928).

Helena Rutherfurd Ely (d. 1920) had a garden named Meadowburn Farm in Warwick, New York. She wrote several books about it, including *A Woman's Hardy Garden* (1903), *Another Hardy Garden Book* (1905), and *The Practical Flower Garden* (1911). She was a founder of the Garden Club of America in 1913.

Helen Ashe Hays (Mrs. W. J. Hays) lived in California before moving to Maryland. She wrote "Garden Letters" for the *New York Evening Post*. Her many books include *The Princess Idleways* (1879), *The Adventures of Prince Lazybones* (1884), *Castle Comfort* (1885), and *A Little Maryland Garden* (1909).

Anna Gilman Hill (Mrs. Robert C. Hill; b. 1872) had a famous garden named Niederhurst in Sneden's Landing on the Hudson River, which was first planted by her mother, Mrs. Winthrop Gilman. She summered in East Hampton, where she had a gray garden of four acres, described in *Forty Years of Gardening* (1938).

❧

Frances Kinsley Hutchinson (b. 1857) was born in Baltimore. In *Our Country Home* (1907) she wrote about her garden named Wychwood in Lake Geneva, Wisconsin. It was designed by J. C. Olmsted in 1901. The home and garden of Frances and Charles Hutchinson, a trustee of the University of Chicago, were on seventy-two acres. They founded the Lake Geneva Garden Club. Her other books include *Motoring in the Balkans* (1909), *Our Country Life* (1912), and *Wychwood: The History of an Idea* (1928).

❧

Mrs. Francis King (Louisa Yeomans King; 1863–1948) had a formal garden named The Orchards in Alma, Michigan. She was one of the founders of the Garden Club of America in 1913, and of the Woman's National Farm and Garden Association in 1914. As well as being a garden editor for *McCall's*, she wrote many garden books, including *The Well-Considered Garden* (1915), *The Little Garden* (1921), *Pages from a Garden Note-book* (1921), *Variety in the Little Garden* (1923), *Chronicles of the Garden* (1925), *The Flower Garden Day by Day* (1927), *The Beginner's Garden* (1927), *The Gardener's Colour Book* with John Fothergill (1929), and *From a New Garden* (1930).

❧

J. (John) Horace McFarland (1859–1948) wrote about his two-and-a-half-acre garden at Breeze Hill in Harrisburg, Pennsylvania. He was a rose grower, nurseryman, conservationist, writer, photographer, editor, and publisher. In 1905 he campaigned for the preservation of Niagara Falls and in 1911 for the preservation of the national parks. For twenty-eight years he was editor of the *American Rose Annual*. His books include *Getting Acquainted with Trees* (1904), *My Growing Garden* (1915), *Planting the Home Grounds* (1915), *The Rose in America* (1923), *Garden Bulbs in Color* (1938), and *Memoirs of a Rose Man* (1949).

❧

Eleanor Perényi (b. 1918) was born in Washington, D.C. She grew up in Europe, China, and the West Indies, and has also lived in Hungary. The garden she describes in *Green Thoughts* (1981) is in Stonington, Connecticut. She is a former managing editor of *Mademoiselle* and has written for many magazines, including the *Atlantic Monthly, Harper's, Esquire,* and *Harper's Bazaar*. Her books include *More Was Lost* (1946) and *Liszt: The Artist as Romantic Hero* (1974).

Hanna Rion (Verbeck; 1875–1924) had a garden of several acres in the Wallkill Valley in Ulster County, New York. Her two books about it, *The Garden in the Wilderness*, published under the pseudonym "A Hermit" (1909), and *Let's Make a Flower Garden* (1912), have illustrations by her and her husband, Frank Verbeck. Her other book is *Fate and a Marionette* (1923).

※

Louise Shelton (1867–1934) lived in Morristown, New Jersey. Her books include *Beautiful Gardens in America* (1915), *Continuous Bloom in America* (1915), and *The Seasons in a Flower Garden* (1926).

※

Mrs. Theodore Thomas (Rose Fay; 1852–1929) wrote *Our Mountain Garden* (1904), in which she describes the garden she made with her husband on a mountainside on twenty-five acres. It looked toward Mount Lafayette in the Franconia Mountains in New Hampshire, and was named Felsengarten, or garden of rocks. Her other book is *Memoirs of Theodore Thomas*.

※

Candace Thurber Wheeler (1827–1923) was a fabric and wallpaper designer and a founder of the Society of Decorative Arts. With her brother Francis B. Thurber, a wholesale grocer, she founded Onteora Park, originally named Lotus Land, near Tannersville, New York, in the Catskill Mountains. Although she had a home on Long Island, her book *Content in a Garden* (1901) describes her garden in the Catskills at her house named Penny Royal. Her other books include *Principles of Home Design* (1903), *Yesterdays in a Busy Life* (1918), and *The Development of Embroidery in America* (1921).

※

Katharine S. White (1892–1977) began working at *The New Yorker* in 1925, the year it was founded. She was a fiction editor until 1958, at which time she began a series of fourteen pieces on gardening for the magazine, which were published between 1958 and 1970. They later appeared in book form in *Onward and Upward in the Garden* (1979). She was married to the writer E. B. White, with whom she maintained a house and garden in North Brooklin on the coast of Maine.

※

Mabel Osgood Wright (1859–1934) was a nature writer and novelist who was influential in the founding of the Connecticut Audubon Society. In her book *The Garden of a Commuter's Wife*, published under the pseudonym "The Gardener" (1901), she writes about her garden in Fairfield, Connecticut.

Her other books include *Citizen Bird* (1897), *People of the Whirlpool* (1903), *The Friendship of Nature* (1906), *The Garden, You, and I*, published under the pseudonym "Barbara" (1906), *Stranger at the Gate* (1913), *At the Sign of the Fox*, and *Flowers and Ferns in Their Haunts*.

❧

Richardson Little Wright (1887–1961) wrote about his garden of seven acres in Silvermine, Connecticut. For thirty-five years he was the editor of *House and Garden*. He wrote over forty books on early Americana and Russia as well as gardening. His gardening books include *Truly Rural* (1922), *Flowers for Cutting and Decoration* (1923), *A Small House and Large Garden* (1924), *The Gardener's Bed-Book* (1929), *Another Gardener's Bed-Book* (1933), *The Gardener's Day-Book* (1938), and *Gardener's Tribute* (1949).

A NOTE ON
THE ILLUSTRATIONS

The illustrations for *Remembered Gardens* were inspired by the cover designs for the following books:

Jacket (front): *The Joyous Art of Gardening*, by Frances Duncan. Scribner's, 1917. (Signed "'CS")

Frontispiece and page 118: *Manual of Weeds*, by Ada E. Georgia. Macmillan, 1914. (Signed "GH" [George Hood, active 1896–1913])

Half-title, title page, and motifs throughout: *Chrysanthemums and How to Grow Them*, by I. L. Powell. Doubleday, Page & Co., 1911.

Dedication: *Judith's Garden*, by Mary E. Stone Bassett. Lothrop, 1902.

Page viii: *Habits of California Plants*, by Katherine Chandler. Educational Publishing Co., 1903.

Page 5: *Southern Wild-Flowers and Trees*, by Alice Lounsberry. Frederick A. Stokes, 1901.

Page 8: *Flowers of Coast and Sierra*, by Edith S. Clements. H. W. Wilson, 1928.

Page 17: *The Ideal Garden*, by H. H. Thomas. Cassell, 1910.

Pages 22 and 23: *Gardens of England*, by E. T. Cook. A. & C. Black, 1908. (Signed "T")

Pages 28 and 152: *How to Know the Wild Flowers*, by Mrs. William Starr Dana. Scribner's, 1919.

Page 31: *Our Northern Shrubs*, by Harriet L. Keeler. Scribner's, 1903.

Page 36: *The Foundations of Botany*, by Joseph Y. Bergen. Ginn, 1901.

Page 41: *The Practical Book of Garden Architecture*, by Phebe Westcott Humphreys. J. B. Lippincott, 1914. (Signed "I")

Page 47: *A Garden with House Attached*, by Sarah Warner Brooks. Richard G. Badger, 1904.

Page 55: *The Garden and Its Accessories*, by Loring Underwood. Little, Brown, 1907.

Pages 58 and 59: *A Few Familiar Flowers*, by Margaret W. Morley. Ginn, 1903.

Page 61: *Vines and How to Grow Them*, by William C. McCollom. Doubleday, Page & Co., 1911.

Page 65: *Little Gardens for Boys and Girls*, by Myrta Margaret Higgins. Houghton Mifflin, 1910.

Page 69: *Wild Flowers of California*, by Mary Elizabeth Parsons. William Doxey, 1897.

Page 75: *Our Garden Flowers*, by Harriet L. Keeler. Scribner's, 1910.

Page 81: *Studies of Trees in Winter*, by Annie Oakes Huntington. Knight and Millet, 1902.

Page 84: *An Artist's Garden*, by Anna Lea Merritt. George Allen & Sons, 1908. (Signed "K")

Page 87: *English Pleasure Gardens*, by Rose Standish Nichols. Macmillan, 1902.

Page 91: *According to Season*, by Mrs. William Starr Dana. Scribner's, 1894. (Unsigned cover by Margaret Armstrong, active 1891–1913)

Page 95: *The Seasons in a Flower Garden*, by Louise Shelton. Scribner's, 1912.

Page 96: *The Poetry of Plants*, by Hugh Macmillan. Isbister, 1902.

Page 99: *Garden-Making*, by Elsa Rehmann. Houghton Mifflin, 1926.

Page 104: *Field Book of American Trees and Shrubs*, by F. Schuyler Mathews. G. P. Putnam's Sons, 1915.

Page 107: *Wild Flowers Every Child Should Know*, by Frederic William Stack. Doubleday, Page & Co., 1912.

Page 110: *Choice Ferns for Amateurs*, by George Schneider. Scribner's, 1905.

Page 115: *The Formal Garden in England*, by Reginald Blomfield. Macmillan, 1901. (Signed "R" and "T" enclosed in "B")

Page 123: *My Garden*, by Louise Beebe Wilder. Doubleday, Page & Co., 1916. (Signed "DD" [The Decorative Designers])

Pages 124 and 125: *Mountain Wild Flowers of America*, by Julia W. Henshaw. Ginn, 1906.

Page 126: *How to Know the Wild Flowers*, by Mrs. William Starr Dana. Scribner's, 1895. (Signed "MA" [Margaret Armstrong])

Page 129: *Gardens near the Sea*, by Alice Lounsberry. Frederick A. Stokes, 1910. (Signed "GH" [George Hood])

Page 132: *Sylvan Spring*, by Francis George Heath. Sampson Low, Marston, Searle & Rivington, 1880.

Page 139: *The Shakespeare Garden*, by Esther Singleton. Century, 1922. (Based on engraving from *Hortus Floridus*, by Crispin de Passe, 1614)

Page 142: *Field Book of American Wild Flowers*, by F. Schuyler Mathews. G. P. Putnam's Sons, 1902.

Endpapers: *Recreations in Botany*, by Caroline A. Creevey. Harper & Brothers, 1893.

Designed by Jeanne Abboud

Typeset by DEKR Corporation, Woburn, Massachusetts

Printed and bound by South China Printing Company, Hong Kong